TEACHING
IN THE FAST LANE

HOW TO CREATE ACTIVE LEARNING EXPERIENCES

SUZY PEPPER ROLLINS

Alexandria, Virginia USA

1703 N. Beauregard St. • Alexandria, VA 22311-1714 USA
Phone: 800-933-2723 or 703-578-9600 • Fax: 703-575-5400
Website: www.ascd.org • E-mail: member@ascd.org
Author guidelines: www.ascd.org/write

Deborah S. Delisle, *Executive Director*; Robert D. Clouse, *Managing Director, Digital Content & Publications*; Stefani Roth, *Publisher*; Genny Ostertag, *Director, Content Acquisitions*; Carol Collins, *Senior Acquisitions Editor*; Julie Houtz, *Director, Book Editing & Production*; Liz Wegner, *Editor*; Thomas Lytle, *Senior Graphic Designer*; Mike Kalyan, *Director, Production Services*; Circle Graphics, *Typesetter*

PAPERBACK ISBN: 978-1-4166-2338-0   ASCD product #117024
PDF E-BOOK ISBN: 978-1-4166-2340-3; see Books in Print for other formats.
Quantity discounts are available: e-mail programteam@ascd.org or call 800-933-2723, ext. 5773, or 703-575-5773. For desk copies, go to www.ascd.org/deskcopy.
ASCD Member Book No. FY17-6A (Apr. 2017 PSI+). ASCD Member Books mail to Premium (P), Select (S), and Institutional Plus (I+) members on this schedule: Jan, PSI+; Feb, P; Apr, PSI+; May, P; Jul, PSI+; Aug, P; Sep, PSI+; Nov, PSI+; Dec, P. For current details on membership, see www.ascd.org/membership.

Library of Congress Cataloging-in-Publication Data

Names: Rollins, Suzy Pepper.
Title: Teaching in the fast lane : how to create active learning experiences
 / Suzy Pepper Rollins.
Description: Alexandria, Virginia : ASCD, [2017] | Includes bibliographical
 references and index.
Identifiers: LCCN 2016046212 (print) | LCCN 2016057437 (ebook) | ISBN
 9781416623380 (pbk.) | ISBN 9781416623403 (PDF) | ISBN 9781416623410 (EPUB)
Subjects: LCSH: Active learning. | Group work in education.
Classification: LCC LB1027.23 .R65 2017 (print) | LCC LB1027.23 (ebook) | DDC
 371.3—dc23
LC record available at https://lccn.loc.gov/2016046212

26 25 24 23 22 21 20 19 18 17   1 2 3 4 5 6 7 8 9 10 11 12

TEACHING
IN THE FAST LANE

ASCD MEMBER BOOK

Many ASCD members received this book as a
member benefit upon its initial release.

Learn more at: **www.ascd.org/memberbooks**

For Bailey, the most impressive woman I know.
And her daughter Linder, who's just getting started.

TEACHING IN THE FAST LANE

HOW TO CREATE ACTIVE LEARNING EXPERIENCES

Acknowledgments

I'm not sure if it takes a village to write a book, but it sure takes a husband who will feed the cats when you're gone. Thank you, Scott, for waiting up for me when I told you to go to bed. Seeing the porch light on and having you insist on helping me with my bags that I've already carried a thousand miles makes all the difference. Thanks, Tim, for always handling everything else so that I can do the work that I love.

Thank you, ASCD, for being just fabulous, especially Carol Collins and Liz Wegner. You made the book so much better.

I mist up in the presence of great teaching. I'm fortunate that I get to witness so many talented teachers. If the world could see inside your rooms, everyone would know how many great things are happening in education. Thanks for welcoming me into your classrooms and being so receptive during trainings. I hope the strategies in this book further your instructional work.

Introduction

Anyone who has been in education for a long time has encountered a plethora of perspectives and philosophies about instructional practices from leaders, presenters, and colleagues. One fall, a new principal arrived at our building. Our test scores were, well, pretty dismal. And while no one specifically connected the dots for us, a new person was now in our former leader's office. His early pronouncement, which he later recanted, was the following:

Teachers are not allowed to sit down.

In his defense, our school had challenges. It was a high-poverty school with high absenteeism, transience, and other issues. And teachers certainly needed to be up monitoring and checking on their pupils, which is probably what he meant. I have never been a principal, so I can only imagine the pressures they are under to meet expectations from their supervisors and to ensure an orderly school environment.

But when the research is examined about the benefits of students doing more of the active learning than their teachers, expending more energy during learning experiences, and talking and moving more than their teachers, the following guidance would have been more in line with research:

Students should be the most active members of the classroom.

It took me years to realize the depth of importance in that procla-mation. My first year of teaching was marked by covering up my own insecurities and deficiencies. I held an iron grip on my 9th graders, tolerated no dissent from students, and was mistakenly commended by leaders for my classroom being so incredibly quiet. My strategy only worked because our students were quite compliant. What no one knew is that I had nightmares about losing control of my students. I worried about losing my hard-earned job if administrators thought I didn't have things together. Fortunately, one of the most amazing teachers I've ever encountered just happened to be right next door. I watched, listened, practiced, and learned.

My next position was in one of the poorest middle schools in the country. A teacher was leaving in the middle of the year, and I had one day to transition with her. There was no semblance of protocols remaining in her classroom. Her eyes were swollen with tears. Shaken by what I had witnessed, my old control fears returned. I began my first day by posting more edicts than any student could remember or follow. I was determined that these 6th graders would not get the best of me. Right out of the gate, I was going to send the message that this was *my* classroom now. As I began reading these edicts one by one, a sea of blank faces stared back. A stark realization came over me. Only a handful of my new students understood enough English to comprehend much of my decrees . . . thankfully. They were starting over with a new teacher. I was starting over with my new pupils. I erased the board and began anew.

About This Book

This book is about strategically letting go of some of the best parts of the learning so that students reach their learning targets, achieve more, are motivated to work, learn to collaborate, and develop a sense of accomplishment. It's about our students getting in the fast lane of learning so that they are more rigorously productive.

The first chapter is the why—the benefits for students when they, rather than the teachers, are the most active ones in the classroom. Tragically, if the research is to be believed, most students' days are spent sitting at desks listening. Human beings of any age are not very good at that. Learners tend to achieve more and remember concepts better when they can engage in hands-on, collaborative learning. And employers are not seeking students who are good at sitting and just listening, anyway. Instead, organizations today are seeking applicants who are problem solvers, leaders, communicators, and decision makers and can work well in teams. Those skills are better practiced and nurtured in an active classroom.

A myth of the student-centered, active classroom is that it lacks structure. Students need structure and predictability in what is going to occur in the classroom. In fact, one can argue that having effective learning structures in place is even more important in the active classroom than in the teacher delivery mode because students will be moving, working in teams, and collaborating. One theme of this book is the importance of a lesson framework that balances student autonomy and classroom structure. An overarching question in this and other sections is "What content needs to be directly taught, and what can students learn on their own?" Chapter 3 provides some thoughts on rethinking lesson frameworks to ensure that each lesson component has a purposeful, distinct mission. A conversation to have during this portion of the reading is, Are current lesson planning templates encouraging active learning or inadvertently limiting teacher (and student) creativity?

The center of the book is the "how" of getting students to do more of the thinking and working. These are next-day implementable strategies coupled with the research behind them. The wonderful world of sorting offers hands-on, thought-provoking ways to get every student authentically engaged. Station teaching, cooperative learning, and menus provide students with more responsibility for their learning. A common element in this section is increasing student autonomy and internal motivation to work hard. These middle chapters provide explicit strategies that will move students to authentically participate.

The active classroom is not about teachers working less than students or vice versa . . . both sides work hard. But the work looks different. It's more about creating learning experiences differently so that students engage in exploration of the content themselves. It's about students reaching explicit targets in different ways. Within the lesson framework, there is variety, which encourages curiosity and memory. And while there are many times that teacher delivery is essential for parts of the content, teachers also let go, giving learners more control and some decision making over their own learning. The results can be getting more student effort and a higher quality of work.

1

Why Active Learning Matters

Standards. Pacing guides. Textbooks the size of an 11-year-old. High-stakes tests. Changing teacher evaluation tools. A tremendous amount of responsibility and accountability rests on educators' shoulders. The weight and pace of the curriculum loom. All of those learning targets and so little time—how can all of this content in teachers' brains and resources be successfully transmitted to students' heads?

So, we go home and read and annotate. We synthesize and carefully prioritize gathered information. Systematically, we decide what to leave in and what to leave out. We summarize difficult information into our own concise language. A presentation emerges, complete with perfectly cropped pictures that enhance the content story. We have created evidence of solid progress of our learning target. Our work is then pushed out to students, who are clearly underwhelmed by our late-night efforts on their behalves. Students take notes and nod. At the end of the week, students take a test and largely repeat the information back. Once again, we have inadvertently outworked, outthought, outparticipated, and probably even outlearned our students.

They sit. We stand. We talk. They stare. Our feet hurt. Theirs seem fine.

This book is about getting more out of our students. More connectivity to the content. More purposeful, visible, active work that demonstrates progress on learning targets. More student autonomy, more critical thinking, more effective communication, more reasoning. It's also about thinking about work differently. Because sharing a sticky note plot summary with a partner is work—it's just such engaging work that every student will likely jump in. Creating a press release of new lunchroom options is work—it's just relevant work. Sorting fractions from smallest to largest with a partner is work, too—it's just fun work. Rolling a cube with thought-provoking economic questions with a team is also work—it just happens to be something all of our students typically love doing. That four-letter word "work" can actually be most rewarding.

Shifting more active academic autonomy onto students' shoulders requires a different type of work on our parts, too. One of the most thoughtful decisions in creating lessons in which students are the most active participants in the learning process is deciding what needs to be explicitly taught to be successful and what students can develop and create on their own. With this movement to more active, student-centered learning is the tenet that students are not just learners but also collectors and presenters of evidence. They communicate with us via their ongoing, minute-by-minute work. "Here is where I am on this learning target. Where do I need to go from here?" And their work—their evidence of learning—should change over the course of a lesson, from emerging knowledge in the opening minutes to a deeper understanding at the close.

The phrase "active learning" or "student-centered learning" can potentially conjure images of an unguided classroom in which students are sort of figuring everything out on their own, but it's quite the opposite. In fact, according to Kirschner, Sweller, and Clark (2006), instruction that is too unguided and does not provide critical pieces that students need to learn can be counterproductive and even reduce achievement. The strategies employed in this book fit into an instructional framework that thoughtfully builds time at appropriate junctures for students to process what they are learning. Throughout the lesson, students' work will visibly develop and deepen, and by the end of class, all students will have something to "show" for their work today. Creating more active learners does not imply that we are less active as teachers. It's about creating a balance between teachers' roles in learning and our students' responsibilities.

And while this book is largely focused on the "how" part of getting students actively involved in their work, it's important to begin with some of the "whys" because many short- and long-term benefits can be gleaned from pivoting to a more student-centered classroom.

Active Student Learning Can Lead to Higher Achievement

Definitions abound for both "active learning" and "student-centered learning," but a central theme is this: Less time and focus are allocated for teacher presentation (and talking in general), and a greater emphasis and time are spent on having students develop, read, solve, create, analyze, and summarize—and a larger share of those rigorous verbs falls on students' capable shoulders. In a traditional classroom, information largely flows from teacher to students. Teachers are highly engaged as they move, write, explain, erase, question, rephrase, and answer. In an active, student-centered classroom, information flows in both directions, and students are highly active. They are not passive receivers of information. Additionally, lessons are created with designated work time for students to absorb, collaborate, and create, so that students actively working takes a bigger piece of class time than teacher presentation.

Teacher talk time is a problem. Hattie (2012) indicates that somewhere between 70 and 80 percent of class time is occupied by teachers talking and that the older students are outtalked even more than students in younger grades. Researchers Tsegaye and Davidson (2014) found in their study of language teachers that it was even higher, with an average of 83.4 percent classroom discourse belonging to teachers and 16.9 percent to students. This is not a new concern. In 1969, Cross and Nagle discussed the problem of secondary English teachers talking three times more often than their students. But what's really interesting is they cite research from *1912* bemoaning the same problem, specifically that teachers talk about 64 percent of the time, less than Hattie's more current estimations. The question of whether teachers are talking at a higher percentage today than in 1912 makes for interesting discussion but is not the biggest concern. The more troubling aspect is that students *as a group* only own somewhere around 16.9–36 percent of the talking. With that talk being divided by, say, 28 students in a class, the amount that students are getting to talk about their learning is so minimal that it puts into question our entire instructional framework.

The trouble with an imbalance of teacher-student talk is what happens to learning. In a very interesting study by Gad Yair (2000), 865 students in grades 6–12 in all academic content areas wore wristwatches programmed to beep throughout the day. When the watches beeped, students responded to questions about what they were doing: their level of engagement, mood, and thoughts. Not surprisingly, there was a direct connection between levels of student engagement and instructional methods. The lowest level of engagement, 54.4 percent, was when teachers were talking (p. 256). Even though lecture was the least engaging, it was actually the dominant delivery method (p. 259).

In contrast, students were the most engaged when they were working in labs (73.7 percent) and in groups (73 percent) (Yair, 2000, p. 256). Even though these methods yielded the highest engagement levels, they were the least prevalent, only 8 percent of the time (p. 260). So, the methods that worked the best for learners were used the least, and the method that was the least engaging was used the most.

Similarly, in a study of 8th graders studying water quality standards in Indiana, Purdue researchers found that hands-on, problem-based learning yielded greater student success (Riskowski, Todd, Wee, Dark, & Harbor, 2009). Eighth graders were all taught the same science standards on water quality but with different methods. Half of the 8th graders participated in a more traditionally taught lesson that was roughly 60 percent lecture, 20 percent handouts, and a final project worth 20 percent. The other group of students experienced a more active approach, with less than 10 percent of their time listening to teachers talk. The bulk of the active group's time was spent working in cooperative teams designing and building a water purification system. At the end of the unit, students in the active classroom scored an average of 77 points on a 100-point exam. The traditionally taught class scored an average of 57. An encouraging aspect of their study was the broad spectrum of students positively influenced: Traditionally underperforming students, including English language learners, shared in this rise.

But what about older students? They're able to learn material by sitting still and listening, right? In an analysis of 225 studies on active versus lecture-type classrooms in science, technology, engineering, and mathematics (STEM) undergrad college courses, researchers in a 2014 issue of the *Proceedings of the National Academy of Sciences* (Freeman et al., 2014) made this case: A lot more STEM grads would be produced if traditional lecturing were replaced with more active learning teaching methods. Why? Because failure rates and test scores varied significantly between the two instructional approaches. Their work revealed that the failure rate among students in more active classrooms was 21.8 percent, compared to 33.8 percent in traditional classes—a 55 percent increase.

Similar effects were reported by chemical engineering professors Bullard, Felder, and Raubenheimer (2008) at North Carolina State University. In a sophomore course with a reputation for "weeding" students out of the program due to high failure rates and low grades, there were two sections. One was taught via traditional lecture; the other section incorporated active learning techniques such as cooperative learning and greater opportunities for feedback. Essentially, the active class broke up the teacher talk, gave students time to process information with others, and incorporated team exercises. Over the course of five years, students with lower GPAs in the active section outperformed other students with lower GPAs in the lecture format class, even though the active classroom had more students. Active learning, the professors suggest, helped boost weaker students, resulting in less failure and fewer dropouts in the program.

Short Bursts Are Better for Our Brains

The unfortunate reality is that students (and adults) can only listen for a short period of time. After that, they are pretty much pretending. Even students in college—students who have been largely successful in grades K–12, have passed entrance exams, and have healthy enough GPAs to be in college—can be truly attentive for just a short period of time during teacher talk. Hartley and Davies (1978) purport that students could recall about 70 percent of what was taught in the first 10 minutes of a presentation but only a sparse 20 percent of the last 10.

When I am planning with teachers in schools, we utilize Eric Jensen's (2005) guidelines for direct instruction (Figure 1.1). These specify that even high school seniors and adults can only pay attention to spoken instruction for about 15 minutes, with elementary students ranging between just 5 and 12 minutes. Placed in the context of long school days sitting in hard desks trying to pay attention to teachers talking, it provides

FIGURE 1.1

Guidelines for Direct Instruction of New Content

Grade Level	Appropriate Amount of Direct Instruction
Grades K–2	5–8 minutes
Grades 3–5	8–12 minutes
Grades 6–8	12–15 minutes
Grades 9–12	12–15 minutes
Adult learners	15–18 minutes

Source: From *Teaching with the Brain in Mind* (p. 37), by E. Jensen, 2005, Alexandria, VA: ASCD. Copyright 2005 by ASCD.

us with some understanding of students' frequent requests to get water, see the nurse, go to their lockers, talk to the counselor, check their phones, call their congressperson—anything to relieve the frustration and fatigue welling up in them. Their behavioral feedback is signaling to us: "We need a break to do something with this information. Please stop talking!"

Understanding the short time that learners can actually just sit and listen to direct instruction creates an urgent need to be thoughtfully judicious about the portion of the lesson that is explicitly taught via presentation. What is it about this new concept that requires explaining and modeling? How can the onslaught of information be distributed throughout the lesson to provide for more student interaction with the concept? How can the lesson be more balanced in terms of students doing more of the thoughtful work?

For example, in a lesson with the learning target of "How can you make or lose money in the stock market?" the teacher mini-lesson might focus on how to read the stock market section of the newspaper and detail how prices rise and fall. This is a complex concept that lends itself to teacher expertise rather than having students just read text. Next, students take the active role to demonstrate understanding of the concept. For example, each student in a four-person group could select a company's stock to research. Next, they would report to their team about what they have learned and make predictions for their stock's future. Now, individually, each student could select one of the four stocks for her own portfolio and make her case. Teaching is still going on as students are working but in a more advisory and facilitative capacity. Listening to their conversations and seeing their work visibly develop provide opportunities for feedback. By monitoring the balance of teacher talk and student talk, we successfully moved more of the really interesting work onto students' shoulders.

Teachers may feel a panicked urgency to push through the curriculum to meet a pacing guide. But if listening to someone talk was the most effective way to learn, well, all of our students would be soaring academically. In a training session recently, a high school teacher remarked that his classes were just too short to do "hands-on" kinds of strategies. But if students can't help but tune out teacher talk after just a few minutes, what's the point in continuing to ramble on?

For male students in particular, who, according to Gurian and Stevens (2004), constitute 90 percent of all discipline referrals and fail and drop-out at higher rates, this martialing through via teacher talk is especially problematic. Girls get bored, too, but are more likely to at least stay upright and continue taking notes. Boys have more of a tendency, due to the makeup of their brains, to stop working entirely, fall asleep, or tap their pencils in an attempt to stay awake (Gurian & Stevens, 2004). The more teachers talk, the more boys' brains tend to fall into a state of rest.

New assessments are calling on students to apply what they have learned, analyze, and explain their reasoning. Students need time in class to authentically and collaboratively hone these higher-order skills. Marzano and Toth (2014) explain that the traditional teacher-centered pedagogy has limitations. Rather than increasing student ownership and independence, students may be spending the bulk of their time just listening. In the traditional teacher-led model, teachers carry too much of the thinking load. If learners spend most of their time at these lower levels of thinking, students may find themselves unprepared for more complex assessment tasks.

Developing Visible Student Work Provides Opportunities for Feedback

Hattie (2009) calls feedback the most "powerful single influence enhancing achievement" (p. 12). After this pronouncement, he expounds on the critical nature of creating learning situations that promote this feedback. In effect, students are giving us feedback about our lessons via their ongoing work. Based on what teachers observe, feedback to students ensues. In the active classroom, we can see their work developing in a highly open manner and respond.

Conversely, in a traditional classroom, students often develop work—evidence of their progress—and place it in a bin. Teachers gather the piles of evidence, rubber band them securely, and organize them in piles. A few get covertly graded during a faculty meeting, with the bulk winding up under a car seat or on the kitchen table at home. Over the course of the next couple of days, the pile at home gets smaller; unfortunately, more piles are developing in the bins at work. By the time they are returned, that learning goal has passed. Students roll their eyes and inquire, "Do we need to keep this, or can it go in the trash?"

It's difficult to provide quick and effective feedback to students in a whole-group setting. Some students may need that additional clarification, but others do not, and we may have inadvertently interrupted every other student's thinking. Similarly, the desk-to-desk model of feedback has drawbacks. First, there is simply not enough time. Students in desks 20-something wait and wait for help. By the time they are receiving feedback, students in the first desks may be in a holding pattern waiting for help again. Plus, this risks communicating that the teacher is the keeper of all information, rather than placing more autonomy on students' shoulders. Conversely, a setting in which students are comfortable revealing their work almost minute by minute provides opportunities to answer the three feedback questions Hattie (2009) recommends: "Where are they going?" "How are they going?" "Where to next?"

Having students work in teams or pairs creates a more advantageous teacher-to-pupil ratio. Rather than stopping at 28 desks, for example, there are 7 or 14 stops. More importantly, students provide feedback to one another. And, with many tasks, it's appropriate to leave an answer key three feet away from students' work area. They can take a quick peek to self-assess when they get stuck. These three feedback loops, self-assessment, peer assessment, and teacher assessment, Davies (2007) tells us, have the power of multiplying the effects of feedback.

In Figure 1.2 from Acquanette Wallace's classroom, the student is self-assessing her work on a math sort. When she's satisfied with the results, her teacher takes a look with her, and the sort is glued down. This

FIGURE 1.2
Student Self-Assessment of Math Sort

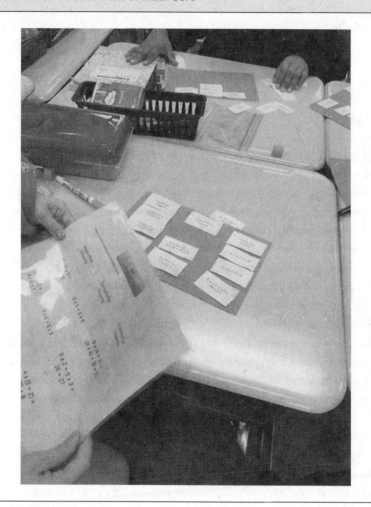

builds student independence and allows teachers to continue working with other students.

Monitoring work as it develops rather than later provides ongoing opportunities to move students upward. In a sense, the work they are creating provides communication to the teacher. "Here is where I am." The work—the task—is what the feedback is about. Here is where you are, and here are some ideas about some adjustments you can make. Their visible work provides us with concrete evidence of the effectiveness of the lesson as well.

Active Learning Can Improve Student Engagement

When one person—be it teacher or student—is in the delivery mode, what's everyone else doing? For example, if one student is at the board solving a math problem, what are the other 27 doing? If one student is reading a paragraph, are the others really following along or just counting paragraphs to figure out when their turn is coming? Are students really paying attention, or have they mentally checked out? Because there is no tangible evidence of learning, it's difficult to assess. Of course, being silent is far different from being genuinely involved—they may be intellectually connected, or they might be thinking about video games.

As mentioned earlier, as students get older, there's a tendency toward even more teacher presentation, despite the evidence that middle and high schoolers can only listen effectively for just a few more minutes than elementary students. Eccles and colleagues (1993) present evidence that there is a mismatch between conditions middle school students need to best learn and stay motivated and the traditional secondary environment; this gap could contribute to a downward spiral in behavior and academics. Some of the factors in the potential mismatch the authors discuss include fewer opportunities for academic decision making by students, less time with teachers, more formalized instruction from content specialists, and the perception that their teachers did not even know them very well. Secondary content has the potential to be grippingly interesting and full of possibilities for student exploration, so transitioning to placing more of the interesting work on students can perhaps bridge the gap between the classroom students seek and the rich content knowledge teachers possess.

In classroom walks, I record approximate student engagement percentages throughout each component of the lesson. When students are developing work, even if it's on a whiteboard or sticky note, it's pretty easy to gauge their engagement and progress. There is something tangible to look at and discuss with students. But when information is being delivered and they are not actively doing something, it's almost impossible. Head nods and thumbs in the air are inadequate for data collection. Plus, when parents inquire about their children's progress, the reply can't be, "Well, his thumb was at a 79-degree angle in class today, so things are looking good."

The encouraging news about student engagement is that the way tasks are constructed influences learner involvement. Hansen's (1989) work talks about tactics students use when faced with different tasks. Learners, he says, are more apt to be genuinely engaged in tasks they perceive as having value and when they believe they have a good shot at being successful in the assignment. When a student encounters a task that seemingly has little value and no clear goal and the student lacks confidence in successful completion, she falls into what Hanson aptly describes as a "learning malaise" (p. 192). But what we see in that student may not look like malaise but, rather, passivity or even anger.

A more active approach to mastering learning targets carries great potential to keep students in the learning game. In a traditional class-room, there are many opportunities to hide—that is, for students to pretend they are learning. In a sense, a classroom dominated by teacher talk followed by a handout or worksheet can be a safe haven for some students. The implicit deal is, "You leave me alone, and I'll do the same." In a more active setting dominated by hands-on, valuable student-driven work, the hiding places are gone. Students have team members who are relying on their work, they are on the spot for a mini-presentation to their group, their diagram is the missing piece their partner is waiting for . . . whatever active strategy is being employed, a highly visible, urgent accountability to the class is present. And, yes, the classroom can get a little noisy. It's similar, well, to being at work.

Skills Developed in Active Classrooms May Be Just What Employers Are Looking For

In 1914, Henry Ford's Model T factory was trying to fill positions for his new moving assembly line, which cranked out 9,000 cars a day. Credited for helping to build a middle class, he paid workers very well: $5 a day for an eight-hour day, roughly the equivalent of $120.00 a day today. Thousands lined up, vying for these jobs. The job trait the company primarily sought: workers who could handle repetitive, specialized tasks all day long (Cwiek, 2014).

Today, employers report that they are seeking quite different attributes. The National Association of Colleges and Employers Job Outlook 2014 Survey asked employers what traits are most sought in new college graduates. With 77.8 percent, leadership skills and the ability to work in a team tied for first. But with two equally qualified candidates in front of them, leadership was more valued. Close behind teamwork and leadership were these critically important skills: written communication skills, problem-solving skills, and strong work ethic.

In 2015, the Association of American Colleges and Universities released an interesting survey that showed a perception gap between employers and students in terms of attributes the students possess (Jaschik, 2015). Only 37 percent of employers held that new graduates being hired are effective at working in teams. However, 64 percent of students reported that they are proficient in this area. Even lower were employers' perceptions of oral communication skills, with just 28 percent of employers reporting that students have the oral communication skills they are seeking. Students who participated in the survey had a different view of their skills, with 62 percent reporting that they are prepared in this arena. And while 57 percent of students perceive themselves as being innovative and creative, only about half of the employers report that recent grads possess these attributes.

Even students graduating from prestigious business schools with MBAs are often lacking the skills that employers most seek. At least, that's the message from Bloomberg (Levy & Rodkin, 2015). Six hundred fourteen employers responded to a survey that queried not just the qualities they sought in candidates but also the attributes that are the most difficult to find. Their results are displayed in a dynamic online graphic called "The Skills Gap." These are the skills employers most desire in candidates but have the most difficulty finding: creative problem-solving, strategic thinking, leadership, and communication skills. (The abilities to work collaboratively and think analytically are skills also highly sought, but employers more frequently report seeing these attributes in candidates.)

What about entry-level manufacturing jobs for students going straight from high school to work? DeLeon and Borchers (1998) examined Texas manufacturers with more than 500 employees seeking to determine the most needed skills for employees with high school diplomas. A large number expressed the urgent need for students to be proficient enough in reading, math, and writing to be able to be successful at interpreting instruments and gauges, reading technical manuals, and composing a business memorandum. Seventy-three percent of employers viewed problem-solving skills as critical. Close behind problem solving was being able to make good decisions independently. But the skill most important at 90 percent? Being an effective team member. And 88 percent of employers viewed pride in one's work as an absolutely essential criterion for employment.

Leadership, the ability to work effectively in a team, problem-solving skills, communication skills, and the ability to prioritize work: Employers today are seeking balanced candidates with a broad skill set. The good news is that these attributes are more likely to be practiced in a classroom that reaches academic goals via collaboration, teamwork, and problem solving. One thing that every one of our students has in common is the eventual quest for employment. And while our focus is (rightly) to ensure that our students have mastered academic learning targets, it's good to know that the career-ready skills they are learning in the active classroom can benefit them in the long term. One can make the case that these skills cannot best be honed in worksheets and handouts.

Beyond the Standards: "Soft" Skills That May Sustain Students in the Future

So much of the school world is short term. After all, we typically just have our students for one year, perhaps even just one semester. Our focus is primarily their academic growth this day, this week, this year. But what happens to them? What skills will sustain them in the future? Do the students labeled "Most Likely to Succeed" actually become top achievers in the real world?

Creating self-made millionaires is never listed as one of the missions of educators, but the research by Thomas Stanley (2000) on traits of millionaires is fascinating, particularly the part about what these incredibly productive individuals were like in school. Especially enlightening is what his research reveals about the lack of connection between good grades and future financial success. High GPAs and standardized test scores, he details, may predict school success but are not indicators of which students will reach the top level of economic success. In fact, of the millionaires surveyed, only 2 percent reported landing in the top 1 percent of their class. Most did graduate college, but with a somewhat ho-hum average GPA of 2.9. When reflecting on their schooling, one of the most positive aspects was that it helped them develop a strong work ethic. School provided the opportunity to overcome obstacles, a journey credited for creating these highly productive adults. They realized that hard work was more important than genetic intelligence.

Furthermore, these future top producers were the students who likely challenged even the validity of the tests they were given and the authority figures who pronounced them to not be as smart as some of the other students. Where other students might feel defeated over low test scores, these individuals had the capacity to disavow the results and worked harder to overcome them. Tenacity and leadership skills were two attributes mostly identified in future millionaires. Stanley's research supports that hard work, tenacity, and leadership are more reliable predictors of economic success than school measurement devices such as grades and test scores. A particular, smaller group of millionaires he examined had very low SAT scores. Within that group, 64 percent credited encouragement from teachers, coaches, and counselors as an important factor in reaching economic success (Stanley, 2000, p. 127). Of course, we want to encourage students to make good grades, and for many programs, high grades are an entrance factor. But Stanley's work reminds us that while our students are diligently progressing on today's learning target, they are also learning the life skills of hard work, leadership, teamwork, and tenacity.

This connection between tenacity and future success is the focus of the oft-discussed study by Duckworth, Peterson, Matthews, and Kelly (2007). A short "grit" questionnaire was given to incoming military cadets at West Point, with the purpose of determining what traits, beyond intellectual abilities, are accurate predictors of success in the academy's rigorous summer training, in which typically 1 in 20 drop out

(p. 1094). Their definition of grit is "perseverance and passion for long-term goals" (p. 1087). The person in possession of this "grit" trait works strenuously in the face of challenges and keeps plugging away when faced with adversity and failure. What they found is that gritty students did better than the nongritty ones. And while all of the students in their study were academic achievers, their research suggests that within this pool of academic achievers, the smarter students might just be slightly less gritty than their peers (p. 1093). As in Stanley's research on million-aires, sometimes those deemed "less bright" exhibited a tendency to overcome that label with hard work and tenacity. In the case of the West Point candidates, grit more accurately predicted completion of the academy's rigorous summer training than any other factor.

Malcolm Gladwell in *David and Goliath* (2013) also talks about a special capacity some individuals possess for overcoming terrible adversity to reach success. An interesting example for the classroom he provides is the disproportionately high number of hugely successful entrepreneurs with dyslexia and other learning disabilities. Richard Branson, Charles Schwab, and the founders of Kinkos and JetBlue are just a few examples. The author poses the question, Were these kids so bright that even a learning disability couldn't stop them? Or did their years of struggling in school and having to overcome adversity actually provide some sort of advantage in becoming successful (p. 107)? In sum, he makes the case that for some individuals, overcoming terrible disadvantages can actually become an advantage.

Developing these so-called soft skills in students is incorporated in many districts' vision and mission statements. These communities hope to graduate students with needed character skills to be successful in the community, create workforce-ready students, and help students become lifetime learners.

The development of traits like perseverance or "grit" may seem like something else already laden educators have to take on, but these conversations with students about resilience, grit, and work ethic are a natural fit in an active classroom. When visible evidence develops over the course of a class, there's something quite important to talk about. As we provide feedback about next steps on their task, teachers can commend their diligence and progress, note something creative in their thinking, and provide strategies for overcoming obstacles. We can pair them with a student with greater stamina for reaching a goal. We can share a time when we hit a wall of frustration and how we broke through. At times, however, our guidance may be to tell students to continue working it out on their own, but we'll check on them later. If we are at the front of the room teaching, the flow of information is from us to them. Their work is more than paper—it's their way of telling us where they are and what they are thinking.

Creating learning experiences that balance teacher explanation and student discovery requires some rethinking about what a lesson looks like and perhaps even the role of a teacher. The professional reward lies in seeing students' work develop and providing feedback—to share in their learning and what they found interesting. The best moments are when students wave off our help: "We got it." Working side by side with teachers creating more active lessons, teachers sometimes ask, "Well, what am *I* supposed to do? . . . They don't really need me right now." Student independence, one may contend, is a measure of a highly effective lesson.

Giving students more academic control can be a bit unsettling at first. Like many teachers, I did not want to let go of the grip I had on my classes. This fear I had of losing control over a bunch of freshmen resulted in a classroom of "cemetery rows" filled with students copying my lecture notes. Whatever discussion was had over the topics was highly controlled and brief. I worked late into every night making comments on their papers to further extend this message that I alone possessed subject expertise, so just sit there and take it. My class was so quiet that we could hear the jubilant noise through the walls of the veteran teacher next door, who taught the same subject. Students poured out of her door laughing and talking about the content. Mine reacted to the bell as if they'd just escaped Alcatraz with prison guards in hot pursuit. Any pleas from my students of "Couldn't we do something different today?" were dismissed. This was what rigor looked like, I explained, with feigned confidence. In fact, my class was more difficult and my students' grades were lower because it was brutal. Tragically, I was commended by building leaders for effective classroom management, but my students weren't just quiet, they were terrified. The leaders stopped by my fabulously talented neighbor's class a few times during that year to tell her, "Your students are getting a little too noisy." Had it not been for this teacher's guidance in helping me view my role differently, I would have surely left the profession, perhaps not of my own volition.

The professional rewards of letting go in a thoughtful, structured manner can be great. After all, rigor is about the level of thinking our students' minds are engaged in, not ours. Our tough work is creating and implementing masterful lessons in which students have varied opportunities to explore and discover the content—to dig in and reach their learning targets. These varied experiences in which students are collaborating with one another, working through trials and tribulations in their teams, and reaching goals will provide practice for the real world. Because employers are looking for thinkers, leaders, and problem solvers . . . and they are sitting in our rooms.

Questions to Ponder

- For students to master the current learning target, what needs to be taught explicitly, and what can students figure out and develop on their own?
- Estimate how much time is spent on teacher talk and student talk. In the next lesson, test the estimate.
- If all of your students were asked today to show tangible evidence of where they are on their learning targets, could they?
- Did you get to sit among your students today and examine their work and provide feedback?
- What percent of your time is generally time spent at the front of the classroom?
- What opportunities did students have today to lead, discuss, or collaborate in today's work?
- Do your students have more energy than you at the end of the day?

2

Mapping Out Where Students Will Go: *Our* Work Begins

An innovative business idea has kept you up for weeks. This new product will change the industry standard, create new jobs, and make you famous. Situated in the bank vice-president's office, you begin your pitch for a loan. "Let's take a look at your business plan," the banker requests. You spread out your spreadsheets and graphs. "Well, this is what I'll be concentrating on for the next hour."

Annual review time. The supervisor asks what your department's goals are for the next quarter in order to meet sales quotas. "Sure. Let me share with you this killer plan that will be implemented over the course of the next 47 minutes."

Congratulations! You accidentally raised your hand and are now in charge of the annual fund-raising dinner for the soccer program. The committee wants to know the action plan for a venue, food, tickets, and publicity. "Absolutely. Here's our essential question for this class period: How many plates, knives, and forks will be required for a three-course meal for 67 people?"

Silly examples of what the world would be like if we just focused on goals for just this lesson, this day, this hour. Students might miss out on the big idea, the long-term goal, the entire reason we are learning this. In addition, learners might not realize the sense of accomplishment that comes from reaching a long-term goal via sustained energy and focus.

And they might not get the deep understanding that comes with connections between learning goals—the reasoning and aha! moments when it sinks in that, "Oh, that's why we learned that first. I'm applying what I learned a few days ago to this new information now."

The Big Picture

In every active learning training or coaching session I facilitate, we always begin with the creation of standards walls, which are concept maps that transform verbose, sometimes muddled content standards into concise learning sequences because active work begins with a clear goal. These become our flight plan, our road map, our course of action for a content unit. Because if we don't explicitly share with students where we are heading, how in the world will they get there? After implementing these connected learning targets, teachers almost always report back the sense of pride students feel at reaching goals and moving forward. When the unit is complete, there's a sense of, "Wow! Look at all that we've accomplished."

Standards walls provide order and connectivity to what students are expected to know and be able to do. The rigor is established but chunked into manageable pieces. One way to think of them is that standards walls are like clotheslines on which learning targets are pinned down for students. Without the clothesline, information would be flying around in the wind. These concept anchors demonstrate sequential learning expectations in which goals are reached one by one, but they connect and crescendo into a larger unit goal.

This importance of connecting the part to the whole is a key point from Bailey and Pransky (2014) as they provide guidance in helping students commit information to long-term memory. They say that when students are confused about the central idea or goal of what they are studying, their brains tend to either frantically search for meaning and connections, which occupies precious working memory space, or zone out and give up on knowing what's going on. Simply put, seeing how the parts fit into the big piece helps make learning easier.

Standards walls take students beyond simply an essential question or "I can" statement for just today's lesson. Dean, Hubbell, Pitler, and Stone (2012) recommend that learning objectives connect to not just future learning but previous learning as well. Additionally, they contend that goals should be specific, but not restrictive, and that both students and parents should have access to this information. Properly constructed learning objectives, they submit, can increase student motivation, lessen learner anxiety, and establish the basis for feedback because expectations are so clear.

Standards walls are a combination of an advance organizer (a road map of where learning is going) and a concept map, which serves to organize large amounts of information. The advance organizer side of the equation introduces new material so that students see the breadth and connectivity of expectations for an entire unit. This communicates a linkage between previous knowledge and new information, which facilitates long-term learning (Hattie, 2009). This linkage to prior knowledge that an advance organizer can provide enables students to acquire information more effectively and demonstrates to students what success looks like (Hattie & Yates, 2014). And these patterns created with these maps generate, according to Willis (2006), brain cell activity that causes this information to make it to long-term memory for retrieval. Students remember better with these patterns. I've seen this in action. For standardized tests, our maps had to be removed from the walls. Time after time, we observed students glancing over at the now empty wall, as if they could still see the pattern in place.

Importantly, students learn the verbs of the standards in the context of the learning goals, which are critically connected to the rigor of the standards. For example, the verb "develop" has a different level of rigor than "identify." This ongoing awareness of the verbs in place helped me tremendously as a teacher. Mid-sentence, I would often stop and walk over to the wall and pronounce something like, "The learning target calls for us to compare and contrast, not just describe. We need to ramp our thinking up on this."

The National Council of Teachers of Mathematics (2014) emphasizes the importance of making instructional decisions on learning goals that are connected to the big math concept. Students are able to see relationships between what they have already learned and where the math is going. Similarly, Hull, Miles, and Balka (2014), in their book on math rigor, underscore the importance of helping students make connections among what is being asked of them today, what is being asked of them this week, and the unit as a whole. They advocate for standards being more explicit about how the instruction is going to unfold. These connections can enable students to realize math is more meaningful and connected rather than simply isolated concepts and rules.

And while math has perhaps a more obvious pattern of skill building and connectivity, standards walls offer benefits to every subject area. In the social studies and science fields, curriculum documents are often so laden with text and academic vocabulary that the case can be made that they almost have to be translated for students. In language arts, students are often developing skills in conventions, reading, and writing during the same lessons. What exactly are learners supposed to accomplish?

A quick Google search for defining rigor in classrooms yields some insight into what educational leaders share as attributes of the rigorous classroom. A presentation by Johnny E. Brown (2007), a superintendent in Robeson County, North Carolina, talks about relevance, connections, patterns, and integration of concepts. In addition, the importance of clear expectations of what learners should know and be able to do with ongoing documentation of progress toward these goals are emphasized. Similarly, a presentation on rigor in the classroom by Assistant Superintendent for Instruction Linda Wallinger (2012) of Virginia mentions drawing relationships between concepts and beginning with the end in mind. Standards walls help establish rigor at the onset of a unit and provide clarity of instructional purpose over the course of a unit, typically weeks. With tests ramping up in rigor, it's certainly essential that we map out and describe learning intentions accurately. Otherwise, we risk creating a chasm between what students have been doing in class all year and what stakeholders are expecting on summative, standardized assessments.

These two pictures of standards walls in action (Figures 2.1 and 2.2) demonstrate the advantages of this global approach over a static daily essential question, where students just focus on what they need to do today. Maggie Heiby and Tylana Miller of Crestline Elementary have presented students with the big math idea, "How do I understand and measure angles?" (Figure 2.1). To reach that long-term goal, students will be demonstrating proficiency in five instructional targets depicted on the

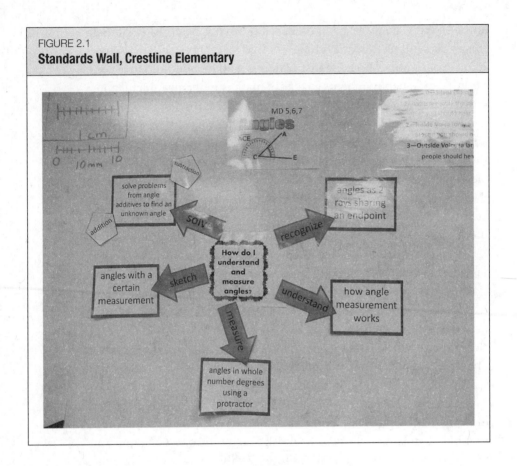

FIGURE 2.1
Standards Wall, Crestline Elementary

concept map over the course of the unit. In these two educators' words, "The standards webs have made making connections within learning so much more meaningful to our students. We have also seen that the students are retaining and discussing the information more meaningfully."

By comparison, James Powell's 6th grade unit wall is quite full simply because they are far deeper into the unit (Figure 2.2). When I walked into his classroom, I knew right away that his class would be preparing for a test. How? Each learning progression had been checked and work posted. More importantly, every student I queried that day understood their learning expectations. That's not to say that every student had mastered

---

FIGURE 2.2
Standards Wall, Oak Hill Middle School

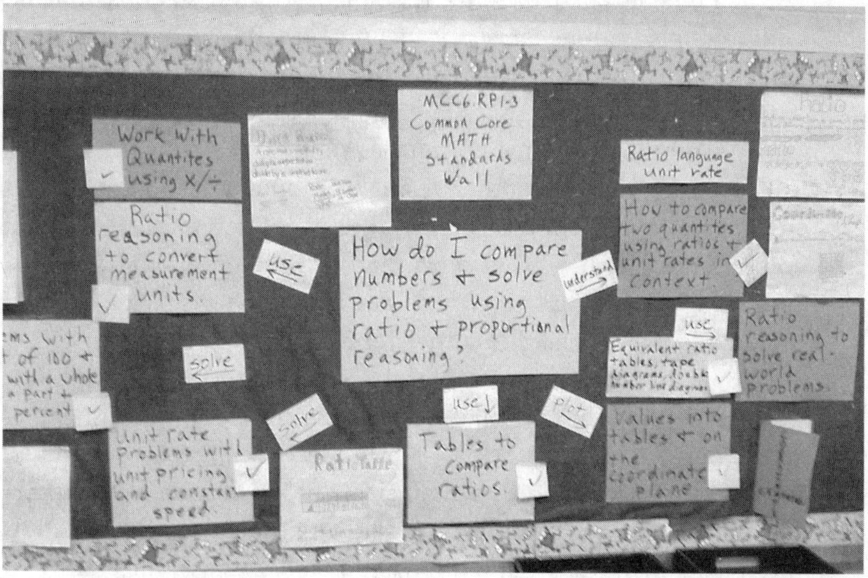

them—or that some targets might not be revisited individually—but there was no murky fog about learning expectations.

Standards walls offer advantages to isolated essential questions or "I can" statements; they provide a more individualized approach to student learning goals. For example, recently I visited a classroom in which students were grouped according to just-in data. Examining student work from two formative assessments the prior day, the teachers created three groups. One, facilitated by the collaborative teacher, remediated some trouble spots identified from their data. The second group, the "almost there" group, required a little more practice. They worked independently but could check their progress with an answer key. The third group of students began the next learning target with the teacher.

Therefore, two learning targets were being implemented at the same time with three different tasks. One essential question might not have served those individualized instructional needs.

In a similar vein, what if the lesson uses learning stations or menus with multiple learning targets? Students realize this via their walls. In the real world of developing effective, active lessons for real students with varying degrees of mastery, it's more normal to have multiple targets in play. A writing station might be one learning expectation, a lab another, and a vocabulary sort another. A single essential question might box instruction in and limit learners. Walls say, "Here's where we are, but some of you may be able to move on when evidence indicates your readiness." It's also perfectly fine to step back and revisit a target.

Standards walls are the cornerstone of active learning task development, assessment, and feedback, so they require thoughtful development. It's not unusual for multiple curriculum documents to merge into one concept map. For example, in science, students are often expected to demonstrate lab safety protocols and technology integration alongside concept and skill attainment. In that situation, the teacher makes a decision on two possible courses: integrating all expectations into one map or maintaining a separate lab safety map and a concepts/skills map.

Here are the criteria to look for in standards walls:

- Are the rigor and intent of the standards maintained?
- Is it student-friendly?
- Is it sequential?
- Is the work posted representative of targets?
- Are students able to clearly articulate their learning targets?
- Are the targets clearly explained in the beginning and end of the learning episode and referenced throughout?

Creating Standards Walls

Standards walls bring learners (and parents) into our world of sequential, connected learning expectations over the course of a conceptual unit. There are no surprises or secrets here. In conferences with students and parents, the wall guides the discussion. Rather than, "She's not working to her potential in science," the conversation can be much more targeted, productive, and focused on student work. Parents can review evidence for each goal and see where additional practice is needed. And from a global schoolwide perspective, it's much easier to see what students are accomplishing in every content area every day. Everyone is on the same page with learning expectations. If student cell phones are allowed in your building, taking a picture of their learning targets (and work for that matter) can build student ownership as well.

Using a California 10th grade social studies standard, the fundamentals of creating these unit maps are outlined in Figure 2.3. Keep in mind, however, that there are other ways to create these. One very effective teacher I observed recently simply put her overarching goal in the middle with "I can" statements in a circular flowchart demonstrating the sequence. What made her approach powerful was not the chart but,

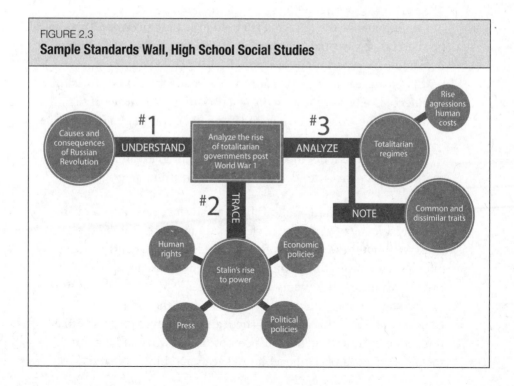

FIGURE 2.3
Sample Standards Wall, High School Social Studies

rather, her commitment to pulling her students into the process every day. My guidance, from years of experience creating these, is to follow the pattern below first and then tweak as student feedback warrants.

Students analyze the rise of totalitarian governments after World War I.

1. Understand the causes and consequences of the Russian Revolution, including Lenin's use of totalitarian means to seize and maintain control (e.g., the Gulag).

2. Trace Stalin's rise to power in the Soviet Union and the connection between economic policies, political policies, the absence of a free press, and systematic violations of human rights (e.g., the Terror Famine in Ukraine).

3. Analyze the rise, aggression, and human costs of totalitarian regimes (Fascist and Communist) in Germany, Italy, and the Soviet Union, noting especially their common and dissimilar traits. (California Department of Education, 2000, p. 45)

Steps:

1. Summarize the unit goal (in bold print) in the center. This can be stated as an essential question, an "I can" statement, or a concept, depending on expectations at your school.

2. Create learning progressions in the sequence of study, placing highlighted verbs—what students will do—on the branches of the map. Summarize the "meat" of what students will be learning in bubbles next to the verb branches.

3. Number or letter the order of the targets. Place an identifying marker, like an arrow, to identify the current learning target.

The use of standards walls as both an advance organizer and an ongoing unit anchor provides a clear road map for learning expectations. Without these, class can feel like an onslaught of information day after day with little content attachment. In their absence, a situation might exist in which students robotically recite the essential question for the day, complete their work, and place it in the bin ("Yeah! I'm done. I'll never see this again!"). Then, another subject begins with a different daily question. Students complete that work and place it in the bin. School can become a blur of sheets and bins. "What did you do in school today?" parents ask. "I couldn't possibly tell you," students respond.

Standards walls provide a structured, connected focus for ongoing work. In the opening minutes of a learning episode, the learning target is explicitly discussed, but within the context of the big idea. Throughout the lesson, evidence of progress emerges. Students can arrange their evidence in portfolios organized by learning targets; additionally, some of these samples of work get posted on the walls. Toward the end of each session, students, teachers, and peers assess where the work is in relation to the target. When it's time to move to the next target, students realize progress and see the marker move to the next goal. A transparent process is in place that provides order and structure for what may seem like an avalanche of information and tasks. Furthermore, these goals can enhance student motivation, according to Hoy and Davis (2006). They report that when teachers set clear, proximal, and challenging yet attainable learning goals, students are more likely to feel motivated to reach them. They continue that the setting of high goals for students and teacher persistence in supporting students in reaching them communicate high expectations for learners.

This ongoing posting and communication of learning expectations was the subject of a two-year project at a high school in which five teacher-researchers sought to ascertain differences this might make to their students. Althoff, Linde, Mason, Nagel, and O'Reilly (2007) found that posting, communicating, and restating learning objectives increased class averages by 13 percent and that students clearly had better understandings of learning expectations. In fact, at the end of class, students were given the opportunity to evaluate where their progress was in relation to the learning goal. In examining three different studies on the effects of goal-setting in the classroom, Marzano (2007) notes the percentile gain ranged from 18 to 41 percent. And while these studies do not indicate exactly how these were posted—lists, isolated essential questions, or concept maps—the critical point is that students were a big part of ongoing conversations about their learning targets.

Standards walls—the concept map approach—brings order and structure to large amounts of information, something Hattie and Yates (2014) say can be hugely beneficial because the mind does not function well with data lacking in structure. Over the course of many training sessions, common questions emerged about developing these. Below are the four most asked by teachers and leaders, with recommendations based on my experience:

1.   **Q: Is it OK to not put every unit target on there at first? In other words, can we build as we go so that there's not too much on there?**
     R: What is sacrificed with this approach is the long-term plan of action—the global view of where we are going. An alternative approach is to create walls with every target but scale the wording down. The opening target will have all the bells and whistles, but the remaining ones will have a bare outline. In this way, students see where they are going and understand that more information will be developed along the way.

2.   **Q: What if students don't know the verbs of the standards, like "interpret" or "classify"?**
     R: Walls assist in those much-needed multiple exposures to vocabulary, but not if they don't know the words. An effective, easy solution is to put synonyms in parenthesis. For example, under our verb "classify" it might say "(arrange)."

3.   **Q: Wouldn't it make more sense to just print these as posters at the central office and hand these to teachers? Why can't students make these?**
     R: Standards walls are robust working documents that we create, write on, and use throughout class. Whoever is creating the lessons needs to be the one who builds the walls. Older students are certainly capable of developing walls, and there is some benefit to that exercise, particularly in building ownership of learning targets. The one drawback is time. I personally would not spend class time for this exercise.

4.   **Q: What do we do with these when the unit is over?**
     R: In most subjects, these are rolled up and stored until end-of-course review time. It's a big deal to introduce a new unit, so I like to just have one unit at a time on the wall. Having said that, one of the

most effective teachers I have ever observed leaves them up. When I was in her classroom one spring day, she walked back to one of the maps from the fall and said, "Students, do you remember when we learned this? We're going to use that again today." It was masterful. English language arts teachers typically teach the standards all year—they are not individual units. For English language arts, we build a wall for conventions, writing, and reading and maintain them all year. There might be an arrow on writing, reading, and conventions at the same time to indicate current learning goals.

Noris Price, superintendent of Baldwin County Schools, has witnessed an instructional change from the use of standards walls in classrooms. The use of this approach began first in math and then spread to other content areas, such as social studies. "Standards walls are an effective way of letting students know what they are going to be learning and why they are going to be learning it." Dr. Price holds that standards walls help provide students with the "whole picture." That whole picture is also instrumental in gauging the district's ongoing instructional progress. When she engages in learning walks throughout the district's classrooms in Milledgeville, Georgia, standards walls help provide a clearer picture of what's going on in classrooms. "I can see how the lesson has been constructed, how the lesson is connected to the big content idea, and why the teacher selected certain instructional strategies to support students in reaching their targets" (personal communication, August 22, 2016).

Removing Barriers to Learning

Creating our standards walls—our road map for learning—is the time to begin thinking about what barriers might keep students from successfully latching onto new material. Are there prerequisite skills or prior knowledge gaps that might cause students to disengage in frustration from the tasks we are creating? Initial enthusiasm for a new concept can wane quickly when students realize that missing pieces from their past might get in the way of their success today.

While we are explaining a new concept, students with gaps may be thinking:

- "This math we're starting seems kind of interesting, but I always seem to mess up when adding or subtracting decimals. I'm probably not going to be any good at this."
- "Here we go again with something about figurative language. Which one is onomatopoeia, and which one is hyperbole? I can never keep those straight. Uh-oh, now she's talking about metaphors. I've heard the word but have no idea what it means. Please don't call on me."
- "Yikes! He just said that we'll need to use perfect squares today. Everyone in class has memorized them but me. Maybe I can go to the nurse."

One way to create this prerequisite list is to answer this question: "My students could master this concept if they just knew_____." The list we create will develop into scaffolding devices, such as bookmarks, cheat sheets, chunking into steps, and foldables. Scaffolding provides a temporary mental reprieve from having to grind back at this critical learning moment and locate largely memory items, such as formulas, irregular verb conjugations, capitalization rules, multiplication tables, biological classifications, rules of citing, or how to use a calculator.

Van de Pol, Volman, and Beishuizen (2010) describe some intentions for scaffolding. Three of those include the following:

- Helping students stay on target to reach learning intentions
- Keeping students motivated and lessening frustration
- Taking over parts of the task they are not yet ready to perform to simplify the task and reduce the student's cognitive load

Donna Smith, a 7th grade math teacher at Whitewater Middle School in Fayette County, Georgia, has witnessed that research in action and determined scaffolding to be most helpful to her students. Specifically, she has discovered that scaffolding "relieves a great deal of stress and anxiety on students' parts. They can concentrate on the learning at hand without being hampered by gaps from their past" (personal communication, May 18, 2016).

There are many things we wish were in the long-term memories of our students ready for retrieval, but that's not reality. Gaps surface for a variety of reasons, including insufficient practice, lack of connection to prior knowledge, lack of relevance, or even student absences or transience. The use of these scaffolding devices does not imply that we are going to stop working with students to commit these to memory. Conversely, we can place something on their tables or notebooks for students to use as a reference so that they can focus on the task at hand. Don't remember what 8×7 is? Check your bookmark. Can't recall which is the y-axis? It's right there on your cheat sheet. Parts of an essay? Here's a sample.

Most of the scaffolding students will need to master the content can be anticipated before the lesson begins. Every year there are students who will arrive without an ample understanding (or just remembering) of integer rules, fractions, parts of speech, or ordinal directions. (Guess what? I don't remember iambic pentameter, types of electric circuits, or physics formulas anymore—my brain has just let those go.) The difference here is that we are anticipating that reality and preparing for it. We are proactively providing what students need in order to grasp new material. Telling students, "You should have gotten that in 5th grade" serves no instructional purpose. (Note that if large numbers of students are rising with gaps in common, that should be noted for vertical planning. Even in that situation, however, scaffolding is still required.)

Figure 2.4 is a multiplication table bookmark, which would be adjusted per student. Because one student might just need the 7s through 9s, and another more. There's no reason to provide more support than required. Scaffolding is typically faded gradually, so that as students gain more confidence and success, the support reduces. In the multiplication example in Figure 2.4, ongoing observations will help determine the appropriate timing for fading. Perhaps the student is ready to remove the 1s through 5s but hangs onto the rest for a while longer. The extent of scaffolding and the rate of fading vary by ongoing evidence of student progress.

These two pieces—creating learning goals in understandable language that accurately reflect the intended rigor of standards and developing scaffolding devices to close gaps in context—get our students ready to

FIGURE 2.4
Multiplication Bookmark

	1	2	3	4	5	6	7	8	9	10	11	12
1	1	2	3	4	5	6	7	8	9	10	11	12
2	2	4	6	8	10	12	14	16	18	20	22	24
3	3	6	9	12	15	18	21	24	27	30	33	36
4	4	8	12	16	20	24	28	32	36	40	44	48
5	5	10	15	20	25	30	35	40	45	50	55	60
6	6	12	18	24	30	36	42	48	54	60	66	72
7	7	14	21	28	35	42	49	56	63	70	77	84
8	8	16	24	32	40	48	56	64	72	80	88	96
9	9	18	27	36	45	54	63	72	81	90	99	108
10	10	20	30	40	50	60	70	80	90	100	110	120
11	11	22	33	44	55	66	77	88	99	110	121	132
12	12	24	36	48	60	72	84	96	108	120	132	144

actively work. These explicit goals lift some of the fog of learning. The goals tell students, "Here is what you need to pay attention to—this is what is expected." Our maps help students filter out nonessential information. The proactive scaffolding piece facilitates forward academic movement. With just a little support, students can still latch onto the new concept. With these components in hand, active lessons can be created that rise to the purpose of our learning targets.

Questions to Ponder

- Are learning targets clearly mapped out by conceptual unit?
- Do targets rise to the level of intended rigor?
- Are learning targets clearly communicated to learners through-out the lesson, but particularly in the beginning and closing minutes?
- Does student work align with the learning targets?
- Is scaffolding largely anticipated and created prior to the lesson?

3

Designing Active Learning: What's in *Your* Lesson Plans?

Picture a brainstorming session at a faculty meeting. Teachers and leaders are asked to generate descriptors of an active, student-centered classroom. These lists might reveal responses such as collaborative, hands-on, thought-provoking, genuinely engaging, creative, teamwork, visible work, rigorous, feedback-driven, and goal-oriented. Now the opposite: How would teachers and leaders describe a classroom that is teacher-centered? Perhaps thoughts like lecture, traditional, quiet, delivery, rows, and worksheets might make the list.

If the active, goal-oriented, genuinely engaging, student-centered classroom is the expectation—the instructional vision—is this being realized in classrooms? A multitude of readings on the subject continue to bemoan the fact that classrooms are still largely locked into a teacher delivery model. Too many presentations by teachers, not enough genuine engagement and work by students. But is the lesson planning process in place driving this active mission or inadvertently recycling the status quo? In addition, is the lesson framework helping students retain this new information that they've been working on or inadvertently contributing to a brain dump at the bell? The purpose of this chapter is to consider the mission of each component of the lesson structure to ensure that lessons drive active, student-centered learning. In other words, what's in *your* lesson plans?

Thanks, John Hattie and Gregory Yates (2014), for articulating some wisdom essential to lesson development and teaching in general: Human beings, and that includes most of our students, are just fine sitting there and not thinking at all. Why? First, it requires effort to think, and we are naturally going to save our limited resources. It's more about allocating sparse energy, they contend, than laziness. Second, there are potential costs to joining in and exploring a new concept, namely, uncertainty. There might be some failure as a result of trying hard, and avoiding failure is a very strong human need, even more than possibly experiencing some success. So students don't arrive particularly passionate about delving into the defeat of the Spanish Armada or finding surface area. Many, like us, are just fine sitting there . . . unless the task in front of them moves them to expend some of that saved up mental energy.

But here's the good part: The way lessons are constructed can encourage students to think and work hard. Effective lessons can move learners to jump in and commit those mental resources and take a chance on success. And how we construct our lessons can strongly encourage movement of new information into long-term memory, so that students will retain it.

Designing learning experiences for the active classroom is a creative, thought-provoking process, largely because the focus is on what students will be thinking about and accomplishing rather than on us. Transitioning to a more student-centered classroom is an opportunity to look at current lesson documents and processes. Are these driving instruction in this direction or inadvertently reining in teacher and student thinking?

Lesson plan templates vary from district to district and even school to school, but they often share common components such as boxes that are completed and checked. The purpose is to have common attributes of lessons across a system or school, an understandable goal. In addition, they are often organized by days of the week, so that a teacher enters Monday's lesson and then Tuesday's lesson and so on.

Beyond that, lesson plan templates have sequential components the district or school has deemed essential. The learning objective is almost always presented at the top. The first component is often an introduction of some sort, such as a bell-ringer, warm-up, or activator. The middle component is where things vary considerably. Some templates simply have spaces for "I do, we do, you do." Others call for direct instruction, guided practice, and independent practice, while some lump these into one category of student work. Almost all call for an ending component, generally referred to as a close or summary. Many include boxes for formative and summative assessments as well.

Pie Chart Planning

I am often called upon to facilitate lesson collaboration in school districts. It's not just an honor, it's a blast. First, we map our unit standards wall and identify scaffolding needs, much like the process in Chapter 2. Second, we isolate the academic vocabulary for the first learning target. We place that on a sticky note for now, but it will morph into integrated vocabulary exposure throughout the lesson. Next, the real fun begins. We take our first learning target—which may get broken down further or in some cases combined with another—and figure out where we want students to be at the end of this lesson. Now, we begin making instructional decisions on how we are going to move our students' understanding from surface level in the opening seconds to competency or beyond in the closing minutes.

For this process, I use outlined pie charts, scrawled on chart paper. Pie charts offer the perspective of time, process, and flexibility within a structure. In a 60-minute lesson, for example, teachers can divide up the pie chart appropriately for each purposeful component. Having said that, it's important to remember that lessons are not bell schedules. One learning target's lesson might warrant 84 minutes; another one might require just 40. Templates with Monday–Friday may inadvertently nudge teachers into artificially squeezing a learning target that requires 62 minutes into 47, or elongate another, just because it's Thursday. Teaching on a block of 90 minutes means that there may be times when two separate lessons from two different targets are taught with a transition break in the middle.

The timing of lessons isn't just about meeting pacing guide requirements, it's about how this lesson will get chunked to match the brain power and attention span of our learners. Each lesson

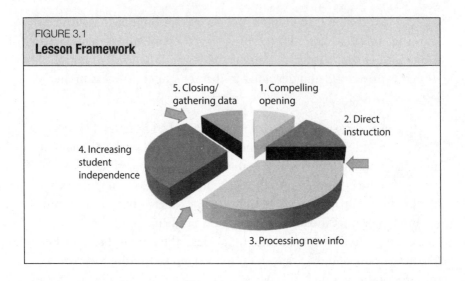

FIGURE 3.1
Lesson Framework

5. Closing/gathering data

1. Compelling opening

2. Direct instruction

4. Increasing student independence

3. Processing new info

component—each task that students are asked to do—should build understanding and move them closer to meeting their goals at the end of the lesson. If a lesson stretches over more than one class period, students need to know where they need to be at the end of the first learning session.

The pie chart in Figure 3.1 is a typical acquisition lesson plan that encompasses the gist of what many schools have on their templates, but it's broken into appropriate time chunks, rather than a list of activities. The arrows indicate ongoing opportunities for quick formative assessments, often before transitioning to the next lesson component. Everything learners do will be in pursuit of the final piece (5).

1. Active Learning in the Opening Minutes

What is the instructional mission of the opening minutes of class? Select from the following two missions the one that most fits your school's current practice.

1. Our mission for the opening minutes of class is to get students working right away so that they get in their desks and on task. This is usually a review warm-up done individually. After that, we correct homework. When that is done, we embark on our new learning target.

2. Our mission is to identify and develop prior knowledge for new learning, articulate our new learning target, establish relevance, and pique intellectual curiosity. These activities are often collaborative, thought-provoking, and designed to further student success in the lesson.

In considering the purpose of these critical first minutes, David Sousa (2008) reminds us of the effect known as Primacy-Recency. Students are most likely to remember what is taught in the opening minutes of class because in the beginning of class, the brain is able to chunk incoming information. But after about 10 minutes, the sheer volume of incoming material makes organizing the information difficult. Students can still learn, but it's harder. Toward the end of class, their brains begin making headway again, and they remember the second most from the closing minutes of the learning episode. Why does this matter so much? Because what is taught in the opening minutes is what is most likely to stick in learners' memories. So by the time students have completed a warm-up and gone over homework, how much time has passed? Teachers may find themselves in the unenviable position now of trying to teach a new concept 20 minutes or so into class, right at the time their brains are resistant and sluggish.

The relationship between prior knowledge and learning has been well established. The opening page of Marzano's 2004 book on building background knowledge declares that the strongest indicator of how well students are going to learn new content is what they already know. Students who are missing background knowledge are more likely to struggle. The good news is that even surface-level knowledge is helpful. Hattie and Yates (2014) tell us that students put more effort into learning when some prior knowledge is in place and that students pay attention to things they already know something about in order to learn more, assuming that the gap is not too big. Students tend to invest in learning when a foundation is in place, and if there is nothing there, learning is implausible. And Willis (2006) elaborates that memory storage is more efficient when there's a linkage to prior knowledge and personal meaning, along with the need to capture students' attention. Bailey and Pransky (2014) expound on this memory component, explaining that the fewer

the connections students have, the less likely it will stick, because these isolated pieces are harder for learners to locate and use because there are fewer neural pathways. In sum, when students can connect to prior knowledge and experiences, their learning and remembering is so much easier.

To demonstrate the urgent role that prior knowledge plays in the learning process, read the following passage. After you have finished, explain what the main character does for a living and what his typical day is like:

> Scooch had worked for years for this moment. What a rare accomplishment to be one of the pelatori, particularly for a Canadian. And while he was scheduled for the matinee performance, he knew that a slot at the evening performances was within his grasp.
>
> It was with such pride that he approached the largest fronton in North America, situated near the Miami International Airport. A jolt of reality hit as he walked past the betting window and a money-fisted patron yelled, "Don't let me down today, Scooch!" The gambling element was something that would take some getting used to.
>
> As he walked onto the cancha, he visualized his plan. There was no one who could manipulate the goat-skin pelota as he could. Scooch adjusted his cesta and began. He loved the shotgun sound of the 180 miles-per-hour pelota smashing against the granite. He glanced through the chain link fence and imagined a bygone time when Ernest Hemingway admired the work of the pelatori more than the gamblers.

How did you do? This is a passage about the sport of jai alai. If you live in the Miami area, you probably breezed through this passage. If you had difficulty with it, lack of prior knowledge probably diminished your success. Did the unfamiliar vocabulary words, like *pelota* (the ball they use) or *pelatori* (a jai alai player), throw you? Vocabulary and prior knowledge are often woven together and can sink students' chances of success before they even begin.

In order not to "jai alai" our students, an opening activity establishing prior knowledge could have made all the difference in success or failure in our students. For example, photos of the sport in action would have been most helpful. Prior to reading, displaying pictures of the sport on a PowerPoint that students respond to or having pairs search for videos on their phones would provide just enough background knowledge to enhance comprehension. An explanation of critical words such as *cesta*, which is the woven basket the athlete wears on his arm, could have made all the difference.

Without this prior knowledge piece, students may become frustrated and disengaged, quite the opposite of an active learner. But reading this passage really isn't much different than some of our students (or even us) listening to an economics lecture or reading a physics book. Without prior knowledge, connections are not made. Learning, in many ways, is about building onto what we already know.

This prior knowledge piece does not exclusively belong to the opening minutes, although for most lessons that's logical. In the jai alai example, students could have been assigned homework the night before to look at pictures online or read an article about the sport. If that portion of the lesson was deep into the period, this piece would be effective just before reading. For students who have been identified as having significant prior knowledge or skills gaps, acceleration is a great option. Chapter 1 of *Learning in the Fast Lane* (Rollins, 2014) provides a framework for this. Acceleration is a structured time in which select students explore the concept before other students are introduced to it. In math, they might read a story about fractions, do a sort with critical vocabulary, and get a little practice. In science, they might identify characteristics of amphibians and reptiles before the core class. Having said that, prior knowledge is such a significant component to learning new information that when I do learning walks, I'm looking for this piece in the opening minutes as well.

The decision about the instructional focus in opening minutes is an important one. One consideration is time. Let's assume that 20 minutes is generally spent on warm-ups and homework review. Pretty easy math: 20 minutes × 180 days of school = 3,600 minutes. 3,600 minutes = 60 hours. Can you imagine having 60 extra hours for instruction per subject over the course of a school year? And too much time spent in the opening minutes on warm-ups can risk sacrificing time on other critical pieces, like student practice, deep processing, and feedback. All of us have experienced that moment when we look at the clock and realize that we don't have time for the last formative assessment—the essential piece we've been building up to throughout class—and say something like, "Where did the time go? Everybody got this?"

Another consideration in narrowing our focus is that this could be students' golden time of learning—what do we want to accomplish the most when their brains are fresh? If warm-ups are an expectation to instill classroom management routines, are there strategies we can employ that get students on task but at a higher level of intellectual engagement, that establish prior knowledge just in time for new learning? Warm-ups tend to be more passive learning by their nature. After warm-ups, direct teaching generally follows. That's a long time for students to be somewhat inactive.

Third, if we are having to spend a disproportionate time reviewing, are there things we can change instructionally that can foster long-term memory in our lessons as we go? Review is important, but is the time we are spending going backward in balance with new learning? A sub-component of that is something I ask many times in classrooms. Does every student need the same review questions? And do we need to review every single homework question or problem? Some students breezed through the homework, and others can't locate it. And do those review bell-ringers relate in any way to today's lesson, or are they out of context? Is it possible to move some of that review later into the lesson to free up opening minutes? And, on a different front, are teachers being laden with too many administrative tasks, interruptions, and noninstructional items that are driving a need for passive tasks right out of the gate to meet those requirements?

If we deem daily review essential in the opening minutes, my guidance is to keep a close watch on the time. In my classroom walks, it's not unusual for this portion to exceed 20 minutes, even in elementary settings. It's inadvertent. Students have questions, they need paper, pencils break, administrative tasks take more time than expected, and so on. The minutes that pass will get cut somewhere in that lesson, which may result in insufficient time for students to be prepared for independent work, ironically resulting in the need for more review and correction time.

Here are some considerations in defining the mission of your opening minutes:

- The learning target is clearly established.
- Students have linkage (or establishment) of prior knowledge for new learning.
- Students' intellectual curiosity and relevance are piqued.
- Students experience hands-on, active, thoughtful learning right out of the gate.
- Opening minutes last an appropriate amount of time, around 10 percent of the lesson.

These openers—I refer to them as success starters—don't have to be elaborate. If today's learning target is to explain supply and demand, for example, here are two scenarios to present:

1. You are the president of the Rose Growers' Association of California. An especially windy growing season has resulted in the spread of mildew to thousands of acres of plants—and right at Valentine's Day! What do you anticipate in terms of prices, and why? Now compare your thoughts with your partner.

2. A popular band posted a video wearing the caps you designed! Orders are pouring in from stores. You've got all of your employees working overtime and are trying to hire more, but it's hard to keep up. What are your thoughts on current pricing, and why? Compare your thoughts with a partner.

Even if students have never heard of supply and demand, they inherently know a little about it. This success starter is thought-provoking, and every student can contribute. In this situation, something that works well is to ask for responses in this format: "My partner said . . ." This encourages listening and communication skills. After reviewing responses is the perfect time to go to the standards wall and say something like, "Well, that's exactly what we are going to learn about today. In economics, it's referred to as 'supply and demand.'" This tees up the mini-lesson perfectly. Now students are ready to learn more about something they have an inkling about, rather than, "Today we will be studying supply and demand."

In math, students may have responded to pictures of real-world examples of angles in action or sorted angles by characteristics. Now, the learning goal of "Explain the characteristics of angles with names such as acute, obtuse, and right" is introduced. In language arts, students might engage in a quick write about a time in which they faced a turning point in their lives. "Now, we're going to read a poem from an author who faced a similar dilemma."

2. The Part Where We Talk

Work in the opening minutes activating prior knowledge, clarifying the learning target(s), and creating intellectual curiosity lays the foundation for students to take in new information and attach it to what they already know. The job of the mini-lesson is now to prepare them for a deeper stretch of work that follows by providing them with the information, skills, and tools they will need to be successful. The need for brevity combined with usually a heavy dose of content dictates critical decisions about what is included. There are days that, rather than a lesson, students just need instructions or modeling for labs or stations, which takes just a few minutes. Other days, a longer stretch of time must be reserved for teacher-led instruction.

Even in the teacher talk portion, the class does not always have to be whole group, although that is often the most logical. One of the most effective science teachers I've observed has a unique way of organizing his physics class. After his opener and brief instructions, half of the class moves to the lab side of the room, and the other remains in a semicircle, which is where he has his teach/discussion portion. This enables him to work, particularly on the math, with a much smaller group so that he can readily see their progress. Then, they switch sides. When students are working in a station format, there are usually four stations with one being a teacher station where new information is taught. In that format, the pie chart lesson would show a few minutes for whole-group instructions and then around 7 to 10 minutes for teaching in the station.

Regardless of the format, the ticking clock of students' waning attention span necessitates decisions about this portion of the lesson in which teachers are the most active ones in the class. Teachers are a swirl of activity—modeling, explaining, drawing, and organizing. Conversely, students at this juncture are at their most passive, trying to connect the dots of what we are saying. If the opening minutes are their golden time, this period of class can almost be described as the danger zone. Head nods, thumbs in the air, and compliance may lead us to false assumptions about their current level of understanding.

The mini-lesson should be chunked with small breaks to allow students to process and summarize incoming information. In math, this may include teaching in steps, first modeling a basic problem and then having students solve one problem on a sticky note or right on their desks with wipe-off markers. Now, after checking their work, the next modeling step may be with messier numbers. Then we check for understanding again. In science, students may create their own visual image of the water cycle thus far. Now we continue. If the social studies lesson is about three leaders, teach one and take a summary/processing break. In any subject, students need a moment to jot down a short summary or diagram of what has been discussed thus far and share with a partner. Now, share that with your team. This chunking and checking model for lesson delivery helps prevent overload—we are all more successful in processing information in smaller pieces. And it keeps students actively engaged, even when more of the work is purposefully teacher-centered.

Graphic organizers and note-taking devices are a good complement to assist students in putting structure to information. Marzano, Pickering, and Pollock (2001) show a range of 13 to 44 percent percentile increases when students take notes (p. 44). In terms of note-taking practices, they provide a few guidelines that can maximize student benefits:

- Taking verbatim notes is the least effective.
- Notes are a work in progress—it's a good practice to have students revise and review them.
- Notes should serve as study guides for tests.
- Guidance to students to keep their notes very short may be off target. Let them write as much as they need to understand . . . but again, not verbatim.

Selecting the best graphic organizer or note-taking device, of course, varies by the instructional goal. If the lesson is largely compare and contrast, a matrix of characteristics or attributes is effective. For example, if the lesson is to compare three civil rights leaders, students might compare and contrast them by background, vision, and contributions. (In this situation, the teacher might model one leader, and then students work in pairs on the other two.) For authors, students may examine backgrounds, genres, and writing styles. For a learning target that requires students to explain a big idea (e.g., capitalism), a web might be more effective. If the structure of the lesson is sequential (e.g., phases of the moon), a time line or flowchart might be in order. Concepts like the water cycle warrant process organizers, often with circular arrows. Similarly, if we are largely teaching steps or procedures, students can create numbered boxes with arrows. And sometimes two-column notes or paper folded into fours may be the most conducive. A plethora of organizers are available online. The work here is to adapt them for the learning target and to know how much modeling is required and when to let go for them to continue the work.

With chunking and checking during the mini-lesson, students can largely continue to be active learners. Whether responding to a reading, solving a problem, or creating a short summary in their notebooks, students are held accountable for listening. There's not a long stretch in which they are just sitting. The mini-lesson always concludes with a soft formative assessment. In math, this might be a whiteboard or sticky note problem. In science, it might be to categorize classroom items by opaque, transparent, and translucent. These quick checks provide an opportunity to address misconceptions and facilitate grouping for the work period. Our second gauge for the effectiveness of the mini-lesson is the level of preparedness for the work session that follows. At the completion of the lesson portion, do most of the students jump in to begin work? Or are many confused faces staring back?

Here are some considerations in defining the mission of the mini-lesson:

- Did the success starter motivate students to learn more?
- Is the lesson chunked in bite-sized pieces?
- Are students given ample opportunities to respond to what they are hearing?
- Are students provided support in organizing the information?

- What percentage of students were on target on the formative assessment at the end of the mini-lesson?
- Were appropriate decisions made about what needed to be presented? Was the teacher's expertise well used?
- When the work period began, what percentage of students exhibited clarity of their mission?
- Was the lesson of appropriate duration for the age of the learners?
- Was the learning target advanced?

3 and 4. The Best Part: Student Work Period

The opening minutes are characterized by articulating the learning target, tapping into prior knowledge, getting students excited about learning more, and establishing relevance. The mini-lesson introduces new information that attaches to and expands on their prior knowledge. Modeling, explaining, demonstrating, sequencing, and organizing information are chunked appropriately with opportunities for students to summarize or respond. At this juncture, in a 60-minute lesson, only about 20 minutes have lapsed. But work has been created from the opening minutes and during the mini-lesson. This early work takes the form of soft formative assessments, such as sticky notes, sorts, quick writes, and partner shares, but all demonstrate movement toward the learning target. Even during the teacher talk section, there were brief processing moments that allowed students to organize, note, or quickly express ideas on incoming information.

Students' brains can get a bit restless during the mini-lesson, but that's about to change. Furniture might be being rearranged, groups are formed, and work is ready to start. They are about to sort some things out, practice, process, research, read, discuss, write, draw, and create. The opening minutes and the mini-lesson have prepared them for the student work period. The work period segment might be shaded green because it's all go, go, go for students now.

The phrase "guided practice" is a broad term for this portion of a lesson. Generally speaking, this is the time that students practice and receive feedback before independent work. For the active classroom, however, that umbrella topic might benefit from more specific criteria because practice can vary tremendously. End-of-chapter textbook questions and worksheets are technically practice, but they hardly promote enthusiasm for work. And going desk to desk to 28 students checking on learners is technically feedback, but it's tough to provide ample time for rich feedback in that delivery model. And while the mini-lesson is understandably often whole group, the first chunk of the work period lends itself much more to teams or pairs. This piece of the lesson is the bridge between us talking and them creating independent work. It's also the piece, from a dizzying number of classroom observations, I see missing the most. In the active classroom, students typically do not proceed straight from teach to independent work.

The purpose of the first part of the student work period is to advance student understanding on the learning goal by deepening processing. This is where students gradually hit their stride. They will connect the dots on the new concept through practice, collaboration, and feedback. This is often the noisiest, most active part of the lesson. Logically, this portion of class is going to look different in a beginning foreign language classroom than in social studies. And a new math concept that requires practice will use a different structure than science labs.

However, even with the differences in content and grade levels, there are common elements that promote active learning to prepare students for independent work. Here are some broad items to consider for this period of deepening processing.

- **Make work visible.** When possible, create anchor charts, time lines, matrices, math problems—whatever practice is required—using chart paper and markers rather than filler paper. This allows for easy visibility to provide feedback. Even when they are reading, their pages should be covered with sticky flags adorned with notes. In this way, conversations about work are natural: "Oh, I see that you noted this battle as a turning point. Tell me more about your thinking." In math, this may look like working on whiteboards or chart paper with a partner before transitioning to paper. In language arts, this might be a web on chart paper before students embark on their own individual papers. In this way, we can see everything—their thoughts, their processes, and their misconceptions. Their hiding places, such as students slumped over hiding their papers, are gone.

- **Allow for practice.** *The Art and Science of Teaching* (Marzano, 2007) provides a summary of how practice varies by content. Multiplying integers, for example, is a skill with specific steps that requires practice. Volleyball players spend hours practicing serves so that when they come to the line, it's automatic. This knowledge is procedural. Tracing the causes of the French Revolution, comparing the theories of two scientists, or explaining the power of waves is a different type of work, or practice. So practice is going to look different depending on whether it is skill- or information-based. And one student may not require as much practice as another. Having said that, the practice of practicing, Marzano shares, has a healthy percentage gain size ranging from 18 to 44 percent. Students need practice, but practice is not the same as drill and kill. Students can practice multiplying integers with a card game. Students can roll a cube with problems on it and share their answers. Students can offer guidance to a pretend student in an error analysis or write from the perspective of someone in a math career. Practice and worksheets are not synonymous. In text-driven classes, who is doing the reading during this time? Are students delving in and annotating, or does reading happen in a round-robin format, in which students are boxed into listening to one paragraph at a time? Are students offered multiple sources or only the textbook's perspective?

- **Provide multiple, varied representations over time.** To encourage movement to long-term memory, Nuthall (1999) recommends three to four experiences of the same information over no more than a two-day period. These multiple encounters help students build relationships with the information, enabling them to see things in different contexts. Students need practice to make connections, but there needs to be variety in those practice tasks. He cautions that, although the research suggests that students need to experience information three to four times, simple repetition is not the answer; rather, a variety of experiences is encouraged. Repetitive, boring sameness can cause students to readily forget material. He mentions the overuse of textbook worksheets as one example.

- **Make it cooperative.** The beginning portion of the work period is ideal for cooperative learning. With teams in place, feedback is in loops. In the desk-to-desk model, feedback is largely teacher driven. In teams, other voices and opinions are readily available. (Of course, we need to diligently monitor for misconceptions in teams.) If students are reading about the Trail of Tears, for example, each member might research a critical person or event. They then teach their team. A group task now emerges, such as the creation of a newswire story that covers who, what, when, where, and how. With fiction, all team members might read the same passage but with the task of analyzing separate characters. Now, as a team, they pool their resources to create a character chart. In math, all team members might work a handful of problems first but now share their work and develop consensus answers for the group.

• **Make it feedback-driven.** Feedback, as Hattie and Timperley (2007) remind us, is simply a part of the teaching process. Feedback is one of the most effective practices at our disposal, but the authors share that feedback in which students received information about how to be better at a task tops the list. Feedback is about where students are now and how they can make progress on their learning goal. In addition, they reveal that feedback that connects performance to effort or ability can be quite productive. (Less effective feedback includes rewards, praise, and even punishment.)

The active student work period offers rich opportunities for feedback. Before they embark on independent work, this processing time is perfect for conversations and written comments about their developing work. The traditional approach of gathering up handouts and grading until the wee hours of the morning bypasses these optimum moments when work is actually being created. Looking at it later, well, is akin to calling a tennis player hours after practice and explaining how his or her toss is off. A little helpful, perhaps, but a lot less effective than catching the errors at the time and working together to make the serve stronger right then, so that the athlete can see the improved results.

• **Differentiate.** Scaffolding created in Chapter 2 can pay dividends in the work period. Sample work, cheat sheet reminders, steps in a process, or bookmarks with critical information that students may have forgotten or didn't get the hang of the first time are placed on tables or in student notebooks. These barriers that we anticipated when planning the lesson will be lowered so that students can better concentrate on the work at hand. In addition, text that is shorter, has more pictures and graphics, and has annotated critical vocabulary is helpful. Sometimes it's a matter of writing "Skip this" or "Important!" on some paragraphs for some students to better navigate the reading. Employing multiple learning channels encourages active learning. A map station in which students can trace a route with their fingers, news interviews to watch, podcasts, manipulatives, and historic photographs and music to examine are examples of incorporating the use of multiple senses. Remember that differentiation is also for students who are ready to move on. Very recently, I was in a classroom in which the teacher announced to a student, "You have met the 5th grade math standard. You can move to that group now—they are working on some challenge questions."

The early work period is a robustly active experience in which students peer edit, share ideas, research, practice, and collaborate. This is their processing time, and evidence of learning is clearly emerging. Effective teaching is ongoing, but it has moved from the front of the room to the middle. Teaching is purposefully facilitative during this time: Teachers are listening to students' ideas, clarifying misconceptions, nurturing growth, and helping them close gaps.

The mission of this segment of the lesson often lends itself to teams and pairs. There is safety in working in teams so that students have peers on which to rely. Together, they have explored, collaborated, and developed a product in a team, typically responding to the learning target of the day. For example, if the learning target is to compare different forms of government, students might engage in a jigsaw approach, each taking one type of government, becoming an "expert," and sharing with the group. Together, they create a compare and contrast organizer detailing the results of their work together. Fantastic. The question now becomes, What does each student know on his or her own?

A more confident student should have emerged as a result of the processing/practicing period. If students just learned about the circulatory system minutes ago, the expectation is not to head into surgery today.

However, using their notes and work thus far, they can now articulate their own understandings of the learning target, perhaps by individually creating a flowchart explaining the system. In math, they might have problems to work on by themselves. Working in teams can be highly engaging and give the appearance that everyone has it. But at the end of each learning episode, evidence of progress by each student is important.

Here are some considerations in defining the mission of the student work period:

- Is work highly visible so that we can see and hear progress toward the learning target?
- Is work differentiated? Examples might include varying text, using different learning channels, scaffolding in place, and offering opportunities to move on when mastery is evident.
- Is ongoing feedback provided in a safe environment so that students can meet learning goals?
- Are students given time to practice in a way in which their understanding deepens?
- Are students confident in independent work? Were they ready to work independently?
- Does work asked of students rise to (or extend beyond) the rigor of the learning target?

5. Closing Minutes: Time to Assess Evidence of Learning

The learning episode is winding down, and the learning target is revisited. All of the collective and individual efforts from the opening bell have led us here. In essence, students have been working all period for these final moments—here is the evidence of their progress. In these final minutes of class, it's the last opportunity to assess where students are, provide feedback, and fill in any missing pieces for potential homework. If a learning target extends more than one day, this is a midway checkpoint. For example, if students are constructing an essay, perhaps today's checkpoint is their rough drafts. If the lesson has concluded for this learning target, formative data are being collected with this final piece.

To skip this piece is to forgo the end of a movie or the final chapter in a novel. The lesson is incomplete. In addition, this is the time of class that students have the second highest rate of recall, after the opening minutes. Unfortunately, based on my experience in scores of classrooms every year—and my own practice as a teacher—this is a part that often gets skipped. Why? Time. We glance at the clock and race to the end. We scramble to get our students to pull together a "ticket out the door" that's minimally effective because there is no time left for feedback. We glance at their responses later in the day and think, "How in the world did they come up with that?"

In an active classroom, students have been creating work and demonstrating their burgeoning level of understanding throughout class. There is evidence from the opening minutes, the checkpoints during the mini-lesson, a bulk of work from the early work period, and now individual work. Therefore, the pressure is not as great as in a more traditional class to produce just one piece of work in the pressured last few minutes, because we have been monitoring their work all period. The final piece may be part of the individual work they have already produced, a summary of their collective work, or something they would like to showcase. It is a culminating moment to share their progress.

For example, if they have been practicing math problems, the teacher may ask students to circle two they feel very strongly about and one about which they have lingering uncertainties. If students have been working on making their writing more descriptive, students may choose to high-light a paragraph of which they are particularly proud and one that's just not there yet. If students have engaged in learning stations, they have been developing work for the entire work period. The close may have them examine all of their work and synthesize the learning target into a piece of writing, such as an e-mail to a student in the next class. Students who have clearly shown that they are proficient on their target might have an alternate close, such as creating metaphors.

These closing minutes (usually about 10 percent of the class) allow students and teachers to clarify progress on the learning target. In addition to sharing their work, students can self-assess with "traffic lights"—red, yellow, and green dots for perceived levels of competence—or shade in a bar graph the estimated spot where their understanding resides at this juncture. Some teachers have students respond with anonymous notes on stickies on the way out—"Tell me one thing we need to continue working on." These self-assessments are just a piece of the ongoing assessment puzzle. They accompany student work but are not in lieu of it.

These closures assist in ongoing adjustments to instruction. With all of the work observed and gathered in an active classroom, there is not an overreliance on one piece at the end. But this piece is important because it's the culmination of their thinking throughout class. Data and student work in hand, teachers can make instructional decisions about addressing lingering misconceptions. For example, the next day's instruction could provide

- Additional scaffolding for some students.
- A review station for some students with lingering misconceptions on today's work.
- A fix-it mini-conference to address misconceptions.
- Additional practice at home.

In developing and implementing active lessons, there's a critical eye for what we are doing and what students are doing. Who's doing the reading, the writing, the practice, and the talking during the lesson, and in what time increments? But it's more than that. Their clearly visible work develops to higher and higher levels as the lesson unfolds. And by the end of the lesson, students have clear evidence of where they are in relation to the target.

For example, the opener for the respiratory system might involve students responding to blowing up balloons, a significant underrepresentation of this system's functions but a beginning that taps into prior knowledge. The mini-lesson details how much more the system does, but students have frequent breaks to write and talk to partners about what they are learning. During the early work period, students engage in a paired reading, creating notes on the parts of the system. Together, they create a diagram of the system, explaining how the pieces make the whole work. Now, on their own, they might write about the respiratory system or even tape themselves on their phones explaining the system while holding up cards like "trachea" and "nasal passage." For their close, students might refer to all of their work as they complete an error analysis of a first-year med student who clearly has some lingering misconceptions about the respiratory system. Quite a mental stretch from blowing up a balloon in the opening minutes. Observations throughout this process—the work in front of us—provide confidence in recording student progress on the respiratory system. "How did my child do in science today?" "Here, I'll show you."

Here are some considerations in defining the mission of the close:

- Does the final piece demonstrate understanding of the learning target?
- Are students prepared for potential homework?
- Was there time for feedback?
- What percentage of students met the learning target today? How confident am I in that data?
- Where is student work now compared to the opening minutes?

Sometimes, it's easier to observe noncharacteristics of an active classroom. From time to time, I see lessons written much like this: warm-up, teach, page 57 in workbook. The warm-up is often review with little connection to the new lesson. The lesson is often longer than is age-appropriate with no prior knowledge connection, and then students proceed straight to independent work without practice or processing time (the critical middle piece). Ironically, this lesson would fit into many lesson plan templates because there is an opening, a middle, and an end. In this model, students often are trapped in desks trying to just listen and then work independently the remainder of the time. Feedback is limited because of time constraints and going desk to desk. Many times, the next day's homework review is longer, due to errors and possibly due to lack of practice time and corrective feedback.

Transparent Feedback

When I am a consultant and visitor, my classroom visits are nonevaluative—they are genuinely to provide feedback to teachers and administrators. I do not bring in a long template with boxes to check. Rather, I scrawl a pie chart on paper and take notes on each lesson component. These notes include the learning target, tasks, time used, and the estimated percentage of students genuinely engaged. I take pictures of student work in progress and try to compare that to the target. If I'm having difficulty getting a feel for what students know, I speak up. I say something like, "This lesson is really interesting, and I see a lot of you nodding your heads. Would you mind answering a couple of questions on a sticky note?" We pass out sticky notes, and students put their names on the back. They pour to the front of the class and stick them on the wall, and we immediately get a quick look at where they are. I jot that percentage in my notes. Instructional decisions are made right there by the teacher. Some reteaching might be required, or they move on.

When I debrief with teachers, I share my pie charts, exactly the way they were written, with times, comments, and percentages. In addition, I sort all the pictures of work taken in the building by lesson components and place these in a PowerPoint. Here is what was observed during the opening minutes, the mini-lesson, the student work period, and the close. This provides a transparent global picture of what instruction looked like today in this building. In addition, it facilitates a more accurate diagnosis of the effectiveness of each component. If a part of the lesson was not as successful as we'd hoped, here is the exact spot in the lesson where we might rethink things.

For example, about a year ago, I visited a science classroom. I recall it vividly because this teacher had an amazing opener. He shared pictures of the concept in action and had students talk about their experiences with it. He was such a passionate teacher that all learners, including me, were captivated. The transition to the mini-lesson was seamless. He provided opportunities for students to gather their thoughts, jot down notes, and share with their teams. And then it happened. This 100 percent engagement lesson plummeted as he moved to the work period and employed round-robin reading in the science text. One by one, students dropped off. Their body language changed from plugged in to largely unplugged as they doodled and fidgeted. The teacher's behavior changed in response, calling on students to pay attention, sit up, and so on. Between classes, I shared my feedback, pinpointing exactly on my pie chart where things had changed. Together, we tweaked the work period. Rather than round-robin reading, students paired up, one as a reader and one as the scribe. The teacher first clearly articulated the exact purpose of the reading—what students needed to look for. Sticky notes adorned each page, covered with student notes and pictures. After the reading, students pulled them off and created either a written summary or a graphic organizer with the sticky notes. The teacher commented on their developing notes. Engagement increased significantly with this one change.

So, what's in *your* lessons? A beginning, middle, and end? Or does each lesson component carry with it a clear mission? Are lessons designed for active learning? Or is the lesson structure inadvertently contributing to student passivity? The active classroom has varied lessons within a structure that is learning target–focused. Each component of the lesson strategically moves thinking and student readiness to the next level. In addition, purposeful time increments are carved. Because students need time to work with the content and deepen their understandings. Their work is largely open to all—we can see and hear their progress minute to minute. And by the closing moments, both students and teachers have tangible evidence of progress.

Questions to Ponder

- When creating lessons, do you fill in your building's template just to be compliant . . . and then create your "real" lesson on paper?
- Do current lesson templates encourage teacher innovation?
- Are times allotted for lesson components conducive for the attention spans of students?
- Do openers encourage thinking about prior knowledge and encourage intellectual curiosity?
- Do student work periods incorporate cooperative practice to allow students opportunities for feedback to strengthen independent work?
- When class ends, can everyone in class at a minimum traffic light their progress?

4

The Wonderful World of Sorts

Outside of educational circles, the word *rigor* means severe, unyielding, and strict, not a favorable connotation. In medicine, rigor is a term for chills that accompany a high fever. And rigor mortis—well, let's skip that one. But even within education, rigor can have that feel of long, tedious worksheets cranked out by students with pencil-calloused fingers, all by flickering candlelight. Recently, a widely circulated Facebook post had rigor listed as one of the words teachers were most tired of hearing about. Perhaps rigor has gotten a bad reputation. Because rigor can actually sound and look like students genuinely enjoying their work. Welcome to the wonderful world of sorting: the merging of higher-order thinking, hands-on engagement, and collaboration.

Well-constructed sorts have the capacity to move student thinking to higher-level action verbs, such as *rank, justify, compare, contrast, deduce, classify, connect,* and *collaborate.* And sorts can be tremendously engaging. Students touch and talk as they make decisions about arranging the pieces of the sorts. Time and time again, I witness student immersion with sorts in all grades. Students collaborate about the content, defend their positions, and reach a consensus. They use academic vocabulary in context as they work. They even get irritated if they are not given ample time to complete their sort.

In addition to ramping up their thinking, sorts serve as formative assessments. Sorts are highly transparent and typically done in pairs; students provide one another with feedback, and teachers can readily hear and see misconceptions. An answer key, when appropriate (many sorts have multiple correct responses), can be positioned a few feet away to provide students with a quick self-assessment. Many sorts are worthy of repeated practice; in fact, I've observed high schoolers race each other with timers to be the sort champions.

Highly versatile, sorts have varying instructional purposes, depending on the depth of prior knowledge students possess and placement in the lesson plan. In addition, sorts vary by type. Some are largely for academic vocabulary development, providing ongoing, varied exposure in an engaging, hands-on way. Other sorts are constructed for content practice and processing, such as arranging decimals from smallest to largest. Some sorts establish purpose in reading, while others are designed to pique intellectual curiosity for a mini-lecture. Sorts can also assist students in organizing information. And sorts are readily differentiated. Some students may be provided headings (e.g., Sedimentary, Metamorphic, and Igneous), and others might not be provided those pieces so that they can create categories on their own. One group's sort may have more pictures and less text. Another group's sort may even have a couple of missing pieces they need to create.

In an attempt to rein in the big world of sorting, there are three categories of sorts below (sorting the sorts!). Having said that, instructional purposes naturally overlap. In practice sorts, for example, students will inevitably be using academic vocabulary to explain their reasoning. If they are engaged in a compare/contrast sort on three civilizations, they will be using vocabulary on governments, economy, language, and technology. If they are matching models to fractions, the term "equivalent fractions" will be said many times by students, even though it's not technically a vocabulary sort. With those provisos intact, however, here are broad categories:

- Take a stand/anticipatory sorts
- Practice/processing sorts
- Vocabulary sorts

Take a Stand/Anticipatory Sorts

Students are about to read a research article detailing the main reasons students drop out of high school. Before reading the article, students predict what they believe the researchers will reveal. Pairs are provided **ranking** strips to sort, similar to these:

- Bored in classes
- Absent too many days
- Family problems
- Failed too many classes
- Classes were too easy

If pairs don't arrive at a consensus, that's fine, too. They can sort in two piles, ranked areas of agreement and areas of disagreement. Next, the pairs can share with their table teams. Intellectual curiosity has been aroused now—students want to see if their predictions are correct. As they read the research or listen to the lesson, they reposition the rankings. They can even place the strip on the text where the information is located. Thus, purpose in reading is established, and during-reading strategy is in motion.

If students are about to be introduced to information about the D-Day invasion, students might first rank their five biggest concerns as a general. Next, they are provided information and compare what they held as critical to what World War II leaders believed.

If students are about to learn about Roald Amundsen, the explorer credited for reaching both poles first, students might be posed with this dilemma: "Congratulations! You have been selected to join an expedition to explore the South Pole. Exploring Antarctica has challenges. Rank the challenges below in the order in which you deem most important. Other concerns not mentioned? Create your own strip(s). As you rank these, jot down some potential solutions to these challenges. (Hint: sled dogs for the first one.)"

- Traversing the icy terrain once we are there
- Starvation
- Freezing temperatures
- Disease, particularly scurvy
- Mutiny on the ship

Ranking strips are not just for the opening minutes or pre-reading. These can be positioned after the mini-lecture or reading. For example, if students just listened to a mini-lecture or video on the causes of the Great Depression, students might now rank the causes in order of importance, providing supporting details for their decisions.

Facts and Fibs is another sort that gets students tapping into what they may already know about a topic. Taxes, hurricanes, supply and demand, nutrition, fractions—just about any topic can be kick-started with facts and fibs. If the learning target today is to examine the dangers of smoking, students might sort facts and fibs about smoking in the opening minutes. Students create two headings—Facts and Fibs—and make decisions about the placement of the strips. Listening to their conversations and looking at their sorts provide information about their level of prior knowledge. As the lesson emerges, students revisit their responses and rearrange their sort. For this topic, here are some examples of what might be placed on the strips:

Fact or Fib?

- Smoking kills more people each year than alcohol.
- Economically disadvantaged people tend to smoke more than wealthier ones.
- More people smoke today than 50 years ago.
- When cigarette prices are higher, fewer people smoke.
- It's illegal to advertise cigarettes.
- Cigarettes kill more people each year than car accidents.

Always, Never, and Sometimes sorts are a third option in which students defend their positions and take a stand. This sort is ideal for opening minutes when students have some foundational knowledge, perhaps from a prior grade or from starting the lesson the day before. This sort is also ideal as a thought-provoking quick check right after the mini-lesson, in a station, or as the close. While this example is from math, it could be parts of speech, comma rules, branches of government, parts of cells, economics, or even poetry. For example, "Poems rhyme" or "Limericks are poems" might be included. Students defend their positions, often trying to find exceptions to make their reasoning hold true, such as,

"What if it's a negative number?" Below are sample items for a fraction Always, Never, and Sometimes sort:

- When we divide one fraction by another, we get a quotient of 1.
- Dividing a positive number by a fraction makes it smaller.
- Dividing any number by 1/4 makes it 4 times larger.
- When we divide two fractions, we get an answer that is larger than the original fraction.

Practice/Processing Sorts

The mini-lesson today explains the differences between nonfiction and fiction. A quick formative assessment is inserted to gauge student progress. Rather than receiving a worksheet, students are provided a sort with two headings: Fiction and Nonfiction. With a partner, they review their notes and discuss with their partners the pieces in front of them. Phrases such as graphs and charts, setting, plot, glossary, characters, and index are on strips of paper. In just a few minutes, students process what they have learned with a partner. Their progress is open, feedback is immediate, and misconceptions are addressed before we move on.

Nonacademic personnel, such as counselors and administrators, can use practice sorts as well. For example, students can sort favorable and less favorable ways to handle making mistakes or effective and ineffective team practices. Sorts are safe havens: No grades are given, there are multiple correct responses, and no one is really "wrong." There is little risk in participating in a sort—no one fails on them. They are more like puzzles or games than work. Imagine a faculty meeting that kicked off with teachers sorting concerns in order; what information could be gleaned?

In academic classrooms, sorts can play an integral role in learning. Consider today's lesson in math. Students have just learned the difference between prime and composite (or rational and irrational) numbers. Students dump pieces out of baggies onto their desks. One by one, they hold up the numbers and make decisions about whether they are prime or composite, practicing not just the concept but also the vocabulary. (They can take a picture of the completed sort and text it to their parents!)

Word problems can pose immediate mental blocks with some students. After modeling word problems, students can first practice with sorting. Word problems, potential equations, and solutions are broken into pieces. The combined characteristics of the kinesthetic nature of working with the smaller chunks of information plus a partner make things just more doable. After working collaboratively—just getting the hang of things in this safe, puzzle-like format—students can transition to their own paper for independent work. In Figure 4.1, students sort fractions, models, and problems that are all equivalent. The sort shown here is correctly solved. Students would see this in cut, mixed pieces.

Science is particularly suited for sorting. Rocks, weather, the earth's layers, parts of cells, classification of animals, the phases of the moon—categorizing and sequencing information is fundamental to science. What's particularly special about science sorting is that actual materials can be used. Rather than a paper compare/contrast sort on renewable and nonrenewable energy, groups of students can be provided with bags of materials. One by one, they pull items from the bag and discuss which category the item most belongs in. A bag of peanuts in a plastic wrapper, playing cards with a slippery coating, an apple . . . what decisions will students make on each item?

The social studies world is one of large amounts of information and vocabulary that students need to organize and process. Sorting is an ideal tool kit addition for social studies. The branches of government, types of colonies, prehistoric periods, explorers, artistic movements, religions, leaders and their accomplishments, and geographic regions can all be successfully moved from paper and pencil to hands-on practice. For example, in government, students are learning about state, local, and federal government responsibilities. Students make decisions on where these responsibilities best fit among those three levels of government:

Federal, State, Local, or Overlapping?

- Birth certificates
- Speeding ticket
- Incarceration
- Taxes

FIGURE 4.1
Math Sort Correctly Solved

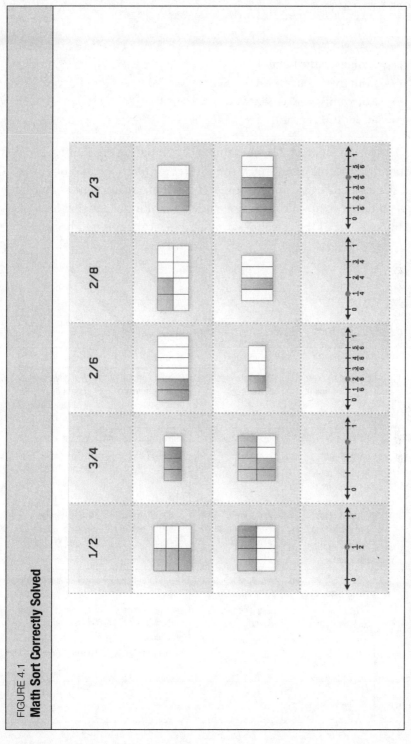

Source: Used with permission from Math in the Fast Lane.

- Broken traffic lights
- Military preparedness
- Auto emission standards
- Snow/leaf removal

The sort in Figure 4.2 is an example of comparing the four types of economies students often study. The sort (correct here) would be cut and shaken before distributed. Students can then create pictures that represent each economic form. For students exhibiting a higher level of readiness, some of the categories can be strategically omitted because students will create these.

FIGURE 4.2
Social Studies Sort Correctly Solved

	Traditional	**Command**	**Market**	**Mixed**
CONTROL	Shaped by customs, not government.	Government control of resources.	Consumers and producers make decisions.	Less government control than command; more than market
CHARACTERISTICS	Farming, hunting. Largely rural. In place for generations.	Supply, prices, and wages managed by central government.	Supply and demand dictate prices.	Market and command. Some protection for unfair market practices.
EXAMPLES	Often 2nd and 3rd world countries. Family- or tribe-centered.	Socialism; communism (also called planned).	United States in late 19th century; capitalism.	United States, France, Russia, United Kingdom.
MAY LOOK LIKE	Tradition determines place in economy. Little growth or technology.	Slower reaction to economic changes. Less incentive to work. Shortages. Everyone gets something.	Higher profits and lower costs. Less government protection for unfair practices. Highly competitive.	Public and private ownership. Lower prices from competition. Government regulation.
PICTURES (Student Created)				

Vocabulary Sorts

As evidenced from the practice sorts in Figures 4.1 and 4.2, sorts of all types can encourage student use of academic vocabulary. They are conversing about declarative sentences, perfect squares, monarchs, or whatever the sort entails. Having said that, sorts can be developed explicitly for ongoing vocabulary development. For example, students can match prefixes or suffixes to meanings, such as "quad" and "four." A variety of categories can be included to encourage thinking about academic vocabulary, including student-friendly definitions, synonyms, antonyms, pictures or diagrams, examples, fill-in-the-blank sentences, and word roots. If the words *ubiquitous, ambivalent, agrarian,* and *obscure* are a vocabulary focus for a reading passage, the sort in Figure 4.3 could be used with partners prior to reading or after as an additional exposure. Students can also create sorts and trade off.

Integrating Sorts in the Active Classroom

Sorts can be an invaluable piece of the instructional toolbox. Sorts can move students' actions from sitting and listening to hands-on, active learning and collaboration. Not every sort, however, encourages higher-order thinking. Placing pictures of cars and trucks into two piles is sorting, too. What moves that upward is asking students to determine

FIGURE 4.3
Vocabulary Sort Correctly Solved

Vocab Word	Synonym	Antonym	In Context
ubiquitous	pervasive	sparse	Cell phones have become so ____ that landlines may become a thing of the past.
ambivalent	hesitant	decisive	Still feeling ____ about which job to accept, she delayed making the call.
agrarian	agricultural	urban	It was a stark change, moving from the more ____ landscape to the city.
obscure	unclear	explicit	The verbal directions were so ____ that he instead relied heavily on the training manual.

common attributes of cars and trucks—now they are classifying. Sorts can provide an avenue for bringing order to information, by categorizing, sequencing, arranging, and rearranging. Sorts can also be a vehicle for student-led decisions, such as in ranking, predicting, and determining if something is never true, sometimes true, or always true. And they encourage students to practice academic vocabulary in context. Plus, they are highly open, safe formative assessments.

Sorts are somewhat short in duration. Whether in the opening minutes, used for practice/processing, in a station, or as a close, they constitute perhaps five to 10 minutes of time. But sorts can deepen concept understanding (Bailey & Pransky, 2014). And learning that uses the hands in this way is more likely to be remembered for a longer time (Jensen, 2005; Willis, 2006). The same sorts can be done more than once by students, depending on ongoing data.

For all students, cutting sorts up and placing them in baggies works well. Some teachers, particularly of elementary-age students, prefer to have students glue them down on paper, after their work has been reviewed. (This requires a sort for every student.) Elementary teachers often have students cut these, shake them, and hand them to a partner. Secondary teachers typically use the baggie approach in groups of two to three, premake them, and reuse them numerous times. For all grade levels, too many pieces can decrease engagement and does not necessarily increase rigor. An important note is that some interactive instructional boards have sorting capacities, and these can be used as a sorting station as well. A potential disadvantage to this is the number of students who can sort on one board. The advantage to having enough sorts for pairs is the level of engagement and the ability for everyone to manipulate and move pieces.

Sorts should be tactically integrated to move student understanding on the learning target. They typically yield high levels of student engagement and are an active classroom "go-to" strategy. Collaborative, thought-provoking, and hands-on, they can be highly effective in the opening or closing minutes, for practice, as formative assessments, and in developing vocabulary. Students discuss each piece and make decisions about appropriate placement. When they finish, they check the answer key and make adjustments. Students realize the feeling of accomplishment of a job completed and well done with sorting. And no pencil and paper are even needed!

Questions to Ponder

- What is in upcoming lessons that can be sorted rather than "paper and penciled"?
- Sorts take some time to make. Are there parent volunteers, student teachers, or others who can support this effort?
- Consider the storage of sorts as well. I place the small baggies in larger ones and label them by units. In addition, lamination is a plus but not required.
- Can a sort be substituted for your next opener or close?
- Can a sort be used in a station rotation?

5

Stations: Something for Everyone

If asked to produce a list of potential advantages learning stations can offer to learners, what would make the cut? Student engagement and autonomy, captivating tasks, increased opportunities to spend time with students, learning through multisensory experiences . . . a good start for a probable list, right? But what about these advantages: reduced risk of diabetes, cardio-vascular disease, and obesity and possibly even improved mental health?

Students often sit on the way to school, sit in homeroom, sit in class, sit during lunch, sit in the computer lab, and sit on the way home. This prolonged sitting has been getting a lot of attention lately, and the news is not pretty. Stanford University held a conference on the problems associated with sitting and reported that prolonged sitting can result in physiological changes that can lead to Type-2 diabetes, heart disease, and obesity. But there's more: This includes people who were exercising 150 minutes a week (James, 2011).

Researchers Owen, Sparling, Healy, Dunstan, and Matthews (2010) point out that schools and workplaces are now designed to limit move-ment and encourage prolonged sitting. Additionally, screen time has increased drastically from greater use of computers, video games, and television, further adding to sitting time. This reduction in movement and muscular activity, they contend, is counter to the human body, which is built for movement and work, and can be quite harmful to heath, including in individuals who exercise regularly. Part of the culprit may be that during prolonged sitting, the body has fewer skeletal muscle contractions, which help regulate triglycerides and insulin. Their recommendation was light activity to break up sitting, such as walking around or standing. Sanjay Gupta (2015), neurologist and chief medical correspondent for CNN, reports that some are even calling prolonged sitting "The Next Smoking" due to the health problems potentially associated with it. He recommends exercising even while sitting, such as twirling our feet. One of the takeaways from this emerging information is that even students (and teachers) who are exercising regularly outside of class may still incur negative physical effects from prolonged sitting.

Stations are not the only way to incorporate movement during class. Students can stand to exchange notes, work problems, or play a vocabulary game. At the very minimum, students can take a quick stretch break during lesson transitions. But stations can be tactically built so that some are standing, such as a map or microscope station, and some are more conducive for sitting, such as writing or reading. Some stations can be on the floor, and some work can be done on chart paper taped on walls. Learning stations, by their nature, incorporate purposeful student movement.

Learning stations, sometimes called centers, may have an elementary connotation, but they are an integral instructional toolbox piece for all ages. As students get older, stations can provide an organizational mechanism for making sense of large amounts of information, often the case in middle and high school. Movitz and Holmes (2007) share their experiences at the high school level integrating learning stations while teaching a medieval unit. A key point in their reflection is that students don't outgrow their love of learning through hands-on, multisensory activities. They witnessed increased student excitement and more meaningful engagement via stations. And yes, these lessons took longer for them to create, but they realized the learning rewards students received.

The Big Picture

Learning stations offer many academic and "soft" skill advantages over traditional instruction. In stations, students become proficient at the learning target(s) in varying ways. Students may work cooperatively in one station and individually in another. For students who enjoy art, one of today's stations might have students cut out magazine pictures to create a collage on the executive branch with a written summary of the art. Another station might have television interviews debating the power of the executive branch. And yet another station might contain a paired reading on "Just the Facts" of the executive branch. Each station has work to do that builds toward the learning target, and there is personal and group accountability. In addition, there might be an anchor activity, such as a writing assignment, that students develop in any extra minutes along the way. In essence, there is something for every student in learning stations. If they are not fully engrossed in the station they are on now, a change is coming right around the corner in the next rotation. Stations provide opportunities to tap into students' existing strengths but also to continue building on weaker areas, too. Differentiation can occur within stations, such as offering a variety of text, or in separate stations entirely, such as a challenge station.

Reasons to Incorporate Learning Stations into the Active Classroom

In many ways, stations are the epitome of the active classroom. In the passive classroom, students are largely copying the instructor's work and repeating it back. In stations, students have teacher support, but there is a high degree of student and team responsibility. With elements of planning in place, stations can be highly successful. Learning stations

- Provide a natural avenue for flexible grouping.
- Allow for more (and better) time with students.
- Enhance student interest.
- Promote varied learning opportunities in smaller pieces.
- Helps students become more autonomous and motivated.

Flexible Grouping

Learning stations provide a natural avenue for flexible grouping. Flexible grouping involves mixing students up into logical teams that change according to the instructional purpose. These team configurations should be fluid (Tomlinson, 2001). If one station involves editing writing, it makes sense to place a student who is very strong at that skill in that group. Similarly, there are times that combining students with stronger reading or math skills with weaker ones makes sense. But some students have keen organizational skills, some are talented in art, some are fast at keyboarding, some sing, and some always finish what they start. And sometimes students can be grouped by interest. Stations provide opportunities to let students' talents shine. In fact, there can be different leaders within one station lesson. Whatever grouping is decided upon for this lesson, it's advisable to have those groups ready to go and posted before the lesson begins. When students adjust to flexible grouping, they understand that the group in which they are assigned today is purposeful but temporary. There will be further opportunities to work with different students soon.

More and Better Time with Students

Learning stations allow for more (and potentially better) time with students. In a traditionally taught class in which teachers teach for a significant portion of the time, have students work independently, and check on them desk to desk, time per student is very small. Feedback is often whole group, calling out misconceptions seen in work here or there or asking if everyone's got it. In stations, teachers can participate in the groups, listen to conversations, comment on work, and provide ongoing, specific feedback. For example, a science station lesson might be broken into three stations: translucent, transparent, and opaque. The teacher can move in and out of the three stations and actively monitor progress. In other lessons, however, a teacher station might be warranted. In math, for example, teachers typically have students grouped in a semicircle or at a table and work with students, often with individual whiteboards. This group is purposeful—every group is probably not getting the same level of problems—and all groups rotate through the teacher station. In language arts, the teacher station provides an opportunity to collaborate on student writing, listen to a reading students have been working on, or have a mini-lesson on figurative language. Therefore, a station lesson with four rotations has the power to make a 28 to 1 teacher-student ratio feel like 7 to 1.

Enhancing Student Interest

Learning stations can enhance student interest. Patricia Wolfe in her book *Brain Matters* (2010) explains that, while a common complaint is that students are not paying attention, the truth is that students' brains constantly pay attention—maybe just not to what we deem important. The brain is incessantly scanning, determining and focusing on what needs attention, and filtering out items deemed trivial or irrelevant. Wolfe continues that one element that draws in the brain's attention is novelty. Paying attention to the unusual is part of survival. (That's why when a door slams or someone walks into a room, we can't help but turn and look.)

Therefore, in creating station tasks, rather than (or in addition to) working on a handout for multiplying integers, students might play cards, with reds being negative and blacks being positive. Rather than calling it the writing station, today it's the bank station, in which students write e-mails to customers about how their accounts became negative and how to remedy that situation. Or it's a miniature golf station in which students have to use negative numbers to calculate golf scores at a birthday party. One caveat is that the goal of learning stations is to become proficient in the learning targets. Novelty should enhance the rigorous learning, not supplant it. But if the same "centers" are used each time—such as reading, software, writing, and practice—things can become humdrum, even habitual, and the students' brains can lose interest. Sameness does not encourage the brain to adapt and change (Jensen, 2005). Novelty, on the other hand, is typically a staple in gifted programs and can promote better opportunities for new learning.

Varied Opportunities in Smaller Pieces

Learning stations promote varied learning opportunities in smaller pieces. The combination of multisensory experiences that students enjoy, smaller blocks of time per task, and collaborating with team members can be a powerful mix. The use of more than one sense in learning helps students not just get it but also recall it later (Willis, 2006). Plus, when students' short attention spans are discussed, it's in the context of things they don't really want to do, like sitting and listening. Attention span is longer when students are doing something they enjoy (Bailey & Pransky, 2014). The beauty of stations is that students begin anew at each center. Their brains get a little break during the transitions, and something new is at the next table to tackle.

Multisensory tasks go hand in hand with stations. Sorts, discussed in Chapter 4, fit beautifully into stations. If the overarching instructional mission of stations today is to deepen knowledge of figurative language, a sort with onomatopoeia, alliteration, hyperbole, and personification gives students an opportunity to work with their hands while classifying. The sort contains pictures, examples, and definitions that students match. A second station might incorporate visuals, such as an examination of short videos and picture books with figurative language, combined with collaboration and written reflections. Students at the third station might read a passage together and discuss how the passage would be altered without these writing techniques—"A World Without Figurative Language." Students could then take a terribly bland piece of writing and enhance it with figurative language. The fourth station may have a choice of two topics to create writing using figurative language. Students would then switch papers and highlight and discuss the examples. In this station lesson, students have worked with their hands sorting, examined videos and pictures, enhanced a piece of existing writing, and created a new piece of writing (with choices). Work is created at each station. In the close of the lesson, students may now develop independent work that demonstrates their degree of proficiency on the instructional target. Students have collected a diverse assortment of evidence of their knowledge of figurative language. They have benefited from the feedback of their team members and teacher. They have also collaborated, created, communicated, moved, touched, watched, interpreted instructions, and reached goals.

This lesson above would have been very difficult to implement without stations. In a whole-group setting, every student would have needed a sort, which would have taken an inordinate amount of time. Every student would have needed a copy of the picture books—impossible. Students would not have been able to provide feedback to one another, resulting in the desk-to-desk model—exhausting. But, by breaking this lesson into learning stations with a variety of tasks, students did the active work.

Autonomy and Motivation

Students can become more autonomous and motivated with station teaching. Carole Ames (1992) examines how task construction and classroom structure affect student learning and motivation. Students are more interested in tasks that have variety and diversity, as well as tasks that offer some personal control, social connections, and challenge. Students' perception of possessing some academic control, according to Ames, can be an important factor in effort and learning. Furthermore, according to Stefanou, Perencevich, DiCintio, and Turner (2004), learners who are provided opportunities for greater autonomy, that is, shared responsibility for learning, tend to develop greater persistence in tasks. Stations, by their nature, are student-directed; there are fewer external controls. Learners manipulate materials, direct discussions, share notes, create, and build. There is an organizational structure in place to manage movement and support work, but within the stations, students have more cognitive control. This increased cognitive control, the authors suggest, is an important component of learning.

Structuring Stations

A lesson plan incorporating stations resembles the pie chart in Figure 5.1, which has three centers. The opening minutes serve the purpose of articulating the learning targets, piquing curiosity, and establishing relevance. The teaching portion is smaller, due to the fact that stations encourage

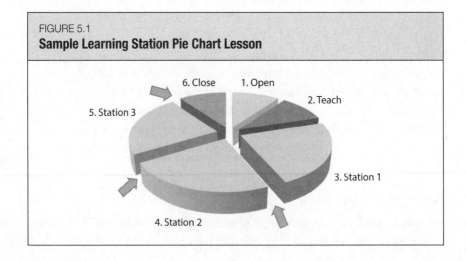

FIGURE 5.1
Sample Learning Station Pie Chart Lesson

more self-discovery. The teach time for learning stations is often modeling, demonstrating to students what they will be doing at each station. (I like to physically move through the stations to show, rather than tell.) The arrows indicate that work will be developed at each station and that ongoing feedback by the group and teacher is a part of the process. The last piece is the culminating formative assessment from the stations. If stations run more than one day—and they often do—these may constitute midpoint checks.

If the lesson in the pie chart was implemented in a one-day, 60-minute session, these are the approximate times:

- Open: 6 minutes
- Teach: 6 minutes
- Three Stations: 13 minutes each with one-minute transitions
- Close: 6 minutes

That sample time line coordinates with attention spans. One of the most attractive things about stations is high student engagement. Physically moving to a different activity brings novelty and excitement about learning. If one station doesn't captivate a student, the next one just might. They can work with their peers toward a common goal and have opportunities for leadership and improved communication.

Considerations for Station Creation

Stations can be highly robust, interactive learning experiences. But they take some thought and planning. Below are some considerations in constructing stations:

- Stations should be designed to show visible, solid progress on learning targets. Does each station contribute to that goal?
- Timing is critical in stations. When creating tasks, each station needs to take about the same amount of time. An anchor activity can be a useful tool. For example, if one team finishes early on a station, there may be additional videos students can watch on their phones, a written reflection piece, or additional practice problems.
- Stations often require some degree of prior knowledge. Implementing stations without these pieces can set students up for failure.

If some students are ready and others are not, a teacher station may be warranted to work with one group first. (This might involve students skipping one station.)

• Stations can be differentiated, such as varied levels of reading passages, annotated text, and tiered assignments. In addition, scaffolding devices, particularly for prerequisite skills, support learners. Examples include a sample piece of work, bookmarks, or calculators.

• Team sizes should be around four. Therefore, stations may be duplicated. So, if station 3 has a video that students will watch, two tables can be set up. Blue team A goes to one, and blue team B goes to an adjacent table. Therefore, for three stations, there are six sets of materials and four students per table. This is just one configuration. You might have seven total stations in a lesson that takes two days. With 28 students, four participants work together at each station.

• Stations should be numbered, instructions should be posted, and leaders should be assigned with clear roles. And while timers are recommended, times should be flexible and based on ongoing observations. Provide leaders with feedback if a team's pacing is off. A minute or so before time expires, it's helpful to prepare students to wrap up, finish their final notes, and begin getting materials reorganized for the next group.

• One decision made in planning is if a teacher station is required. In math and language arts, this is typically the case. (Sometimes the exception is in review stations.) If a teacher station is inserted, is success at some of the other stations dependent on information provided at the teacher station? If so, how will groups be sequenced? Math teachers often create a flexible group of students they have identified as having misconceptions and work with them first and then send them on to stations. In language arts, this station might serve as individual feedback on students' writing.

• Technology integration is often a natural fit for station teaching. Rather than make copies of reading passages, students can access these on their devices. Playing educational games, creating PowerPoint slides, tweeting, creating pie charts, watching or creating videos,

FIGURE 5.2
Sample Station Organizer

Learning target: Explain the states of water and how they relate to weather and the water cycle.

Station	Team Task	Individual Product
1: Water States Lab	With team, follow lab instructions; record observations and share with team.	Draw lab diagram and write summary.
2: Cube Vocabulary Game	Vocab cube game with team. Vocab sort with team.	Word detective: Figure out the missing words from text.
3: Cloud Formation Video	Watch and take notes. Share notes with team.	Create graphic organizer explaining how clouds form.
4: Just the Facts Reading Station	Partner-read pages 66–68. (One reads; one takes notes on sticky notes.)	Arrange sticky notes in order of importance. Write a summary of key points.

examining primary sources—just about any station lesson can be strengthened by integrating technology.
•   What work will students create, and how will they stay organized? A station organizer can serve to facilitate the station process. Figure 5.2 is a sample of team and individual station expectations.

Every station contributes to the overarching learning target for the lesson, but each stop offers something different for students. Here are some ideas that may help bring stations alive.

Writing Stations

Rather than simply having students create a summarizing paragraph, here are some ideas to get students to generate more captivating writing:
•   Create an obituary: An obit for William Shakespeare or Thomas Edison encourages students to talk about just the most important details of their lives.
•   Tweet or text a summary.
•   Create one PowerPoint slide that combines with team members' slides.

- Write from the perspective ("In Their Shoes") of a character, historical figure, or a person using the math, such as a contractor bidding on a job.
- Write a note to a student in another class.
- Error analysis: Students correct errors in a piece of writing (e.g., an article on the Bill of Rights or photosynthesis with all the facts mixed up).
- Write a blog post defending a position.
- Create a press release for the local paper.
- Write one page of screenplay dialogue.
- Create a Facebook profile for a historical figure, author, scientist, or character.
- Write a postcard home from the war.

Reading Stations

Purpose. In reading, an essential instructional component is supporting students in understanding the purpose in reading. This is also true in reading stations. If every station is about the effect the invention of the telephone has had on society, the opener before the stations may already make students clear on their purpose. If the stations are about inventions in general, the prereading activity should commence at the station before reading. For example, before reading at the station, students' first activity might be a scenario in which all of the phones magically disappeared for a week (How would people adapt?). Now students are more prepared for what to look for in the reading.

Tracking. The next instructional decision at reading stations is what method students will use to track the purpose in reading. In the telephone example, every time students see an impact on society, they might code that spot with an "I." (Sticky flags work well for this.) Another option is the use of a graphic organizer. In this instance, there might be four boxes on a half sheet of paper. Readers are going to identify four effects of the telephone and jot down notes in each box. A third option might be to provide each student with four sticky notes, one per impact. They jot their notes on the sticky notes and arrange these in the order in which they deem them most important. There are many strategies that help students track their purpose of reading, such as plastic cover sheets, highlighters, and note-taking devices. These strategies can support active reading. Readers are on a mission looking for their purpose in reading and these techniques can provide tangible evidence of their thinking and prepare students for writing. In addition, as teachers survey the room, conversations are easy. "Oh, I see that you noted that as your most important impact. Tell me more about that."

How students will read. Purpose in reading and during-reading strategy established, the question now is how students are going to read. Are they going to read on their own silently? If so, it's wise to establish stopping points to compare notes with a partner. The length before stopping ranges by age of readers and difficulty and type of passage. These predetermined breaks can increase student accountability—they each have a partner who's working as well—and can reduce cognitive fatigue. (We've all had those moments in which we don't even remember turning the pages.) After the partners complete the passage, the group discussion and work can commence.

Another option is an oral paired reading. One student is the reader, and the other is the scribe. The roles can be switched as the pair deems effective throughout the passage. In the telephone example, when the scribe realizes that the reader has revealed an impact in the passage, a note is made. The scribe may have to put the reader on "pause" for a moment in order to write. After the passage is complete, the reading partners share notes with the team. What if a student is reluctant to read aloud? The pairs can have the option of having one reader throughout as the other student works as the scribe for the entire passage.

If round-robin reading is the method, strips with numbers might be drawn to determine reading order. The during-reading strategy is still in place, however, so students pause to make notes on the purpose of the passage. There are readers who are uncomfortable reading aloud. They may not know all of the vocabulary and feel embarrassed. An option is to assign two readers for the group. The other students can be in charge of materials or note-taking. These students will still glean the information they need from the group discussion and from other stations that have less reading, such as the video stations. This is an advantage of flexible grouping—stronger readers can be distributed throughout the groups. And students who are particularly reliable about keeping materials organized can be spread about as well.

In selecting passages, the primary concern is the learning target. Having said that, some articles can be shorter, some can have more pictures, and some may have more challenging vocabulary. I typically star parts of the readings that are especially important. Before stations commence, I explain that time is short, so a good strategy is to be certain to read the starred passages. I also mark "skip" on some and explain that these are really interesting, but only if time permits. In addition, I annotate quite a bit of the difficult vocabulary. By the word "ubiquitous" it might say, "It's everywhere!" in the margin. These methods, I have found, reduce barriers to learning and even lessen student stress. I frequently say right before the transition, "Don't worry if you didn't complete every single thing at the station. We're going to talk about everything again, and those pieces will fill in."

After reading, students typically review their notes and discuss their key points with their team. Cubes are a vehicle for making learning tactile and highly participatory. (These come in all colors and can be purchased very cheaply online. They are actually mini-sized gift boxes.) In their stations, students roll one or two cubes and do what's on the cube. If students have just read about the core, mantle, and crust, for example, those terms will be written twice on one cube. The second cube will have the words temperature, density, and composition, again twice in this example to fit the six sides. One, two, three, roll! The group sees "core" and "composition" on the two cubes. The two students who rolled the cubes check their reading notes and discuss the composition of the core. The next two students now roll and get "crust" and "density." Cubes can have world leaders, battles, authors, characters, elements of a story— just about any purpose in reading can be placed on cubes. Cubes are a versatile way to make conversations about reading more hands-on.

Making Stations More Hands-On

Cubes work well in math stations, too. For example, one cube might be positive, and one might be negative. Students roll and multiply the two numbers. If students are learning about rounding numbers, one cube can have numbers, like 23,458, and the other cube, 10, 100, and 1,000. Students roll the cubes and round according to what they roll. Plotting points on the coordinate plane? Cubes can be the x- and y-axes. Cubes get every student talking and thinking because they provide a fun, safe avenue for discussions and practice. Cubes obviously have just six sides, so time goes quickly. For that reason, sorts can make a good pairing at the same station.

In Figure 5.3 below, students in Ms. Veal's classroom at Blandy Hills Elementary School are in a station rotation in which they roll cubes with math problems and then solve on whiteboards. A co-teacher is situated on the floor with the 3rd graders providing feedback and encouragement. Ms. Veal is at a nearby table working with students in a small group.

Stations with measuring, modeling clay, labs, maps, and models provide opportunities for students to use their hands. If cell phones are allowed in your classroom, students can create videos explaining the concept, even demonstrating how to correctly work a math problem. Students can make foldables, brochures, illustrations, magazine covers, or bumper stickers. They can make pie charts and bar graphs on chart paper. They can draw magazine pictures from a bag and create analogies with vocabulary words (e.g., high heels are like the Great Depression because

FIGURE 5.3
Katrina Veal's Students Rolling Math Cubes

they hurt if worn too long). Students can examine picture books (which go all the way up to high school) and can create just one more page.

Every station doesn't have to be razzle-dazzle. There can be an error analysis station, an editing station, a software review station, and a practice station. But by the end of each station, students should be able to present their evidence of progress on their learning goal.

Thoughtfully constructed stations offer students dynamic, versatile learning opportunities that are relatable, challenging, and highly engaging. In addition to the academic rewards, stations can promote more student autonomy, encourage effective team membership, and build leadership skills. Students get up and move, have conversations, share their work, read, write, practice, build, and create. In sum, stations are an essential toolbox addition for any grade and content.

An Additional Benefit of Station Teaching

Stations may just offer a bonus benefit to students. Osterman's 2000 review of research on the subject of the importance of belonging to a school community puts collaborative efforts, such as stations, in an additionally positive light. Summarizing the research, she explains that students who feel more accepted at school tend to be more motivated, committed to their education, and engaged. When students experience acceptance and belonging at school, their performance and quality of learning tend to improve. She notes that instructional changes can support not only student belonging but also student autonomy, which can also be motivating.

Learning stations offer the power of pulling students into not just the work but also school. Common goals, interests, and input in completing a variety of tasks provide a canvas for belonging. Consider a professional work environment. Colleagues collaborate, have coffee together, share stories, and work on projects together, creating bonds in a staff. Work would be a dreary place without collaboration, and so would school.

Movement, collaborating with others on a common task, working with different peers, experiencing being a leader, having opportunities to learn in varying ways, and completing an important job: learning stations offer something for everyone. Tactically implemented, stations are a staple of the active classroom in every grade. Students get into the fast lane of learning. They are moving, talking, and creating . . . almost entirely on their own.

Questions to Ponder

- Will the learning target(s) be met upon completion of stations?
- Is scaffolding in place to enhance student autonomy?
- Are stations multisensory, such as sorting, drawing, and listening?
- Do stations tap into varied interests and talents of students?
- Are management features in place, such as leaders, instructions, traffic flow, and anchor activity?
- Will a teacher station enhance learning? Or is the lesson better suited to a "floating" teacher?
- Can technology integration enhance the stations?
- What evidence of learning will students collect in each station?
- What formative assessment at the end of class will demonstrate progress on the learning target(s)?

6

Cooperative Learning: More Than Pushing Desks Together

From 1957 to 1963, Theodore Cleaver, aka the Beaver, from the TV show *Leave It to Beaver*, and all of his classmates sat perfectly still in hard desks with hands folded, hanging on their teacher's word every school day. In fact, Beaver may still be sitting in that desk. In arguably the most famous classroom movie clip of all time, the economics teacher in the 1986 movie *Ferris Bueller's Day Off*, played by Ben Stein, drones on and on about tariffs and the Great Depression as one student naps in a puddle of drool on his desk while another creates a massive chewing gum bubble. Every few seconds, the teacher asks, "Anyone? Anyone?" and then immediately answers his own questions. From the 50s to *Mean Girls* to movies set in college, the classroom is often portrayed as whole-group instruction with the teacher in the front on stage and students passively sitting in rows.

But "group work" also has its own negative connotations. It's safe to say that we have all experienced an unpleasant group work experience. Sometimes, stronger or more grade-oriented students take over the reins of the task, and other group members gradually yield any control, allowing dominant students to do all the work, and then guiltily share in the rewards. Group work can look like disorder, unequal workload, and confused goals. *Cooperative learning*, on the other hand, can be a masterful mixture of structure, student autonomy, and interdependence. Pulling desks together and simply asking students to work together lacks the structure and common goals of effective cooperative learning. Cooperative learning is not just working in groups; rather, it is a tactical, structured, purposeful instructional technique that can have quite positive effects.

Structure Meets Student Autonomy

Cooperative learning is a broad category for small-group work in which students work together to master a concept. But what are the marks of the most effective cooperative learning? According to a synthesis of research by Slavin (1991), cooperative learning at its best has two key traits: individual student accountability and a group goal. In other words, groups are rewarded for good work based on the individual efforts of team members that have contributed to the bigger goal. When these two pieces—individual accountability and group goals—are incorporated into the task, students achieved at much higher levels than with traditional methods. This individual accountability component is critical. Slavin's (1983) research concludes that each student's individual efforts must be visible and quantifiable by other team members. Every student's work has to matter for the group goal. This is different from what might be termed "group work" in which students all do a worksheet, for example, and just sign off on it. Those groups can lead to one student making major contributions, with the others, quite possibly the weaker students, not contributing. Furthermore, his (1991) research continues, outcomes beyond academics can be fostered via cooperative learning, including learning the ability to work effectively with others, more positive attitudes toward school, self-esteem, and acceptance of students with disabilities.

Cooperative learning can create a sense of urgency in meeting one's own work responsibilities in order for the group to be successful, which can be a motivating force in teams. For example, if the team is studying four different cell parts with the end in mind of creating a group compare and contrast organizer, each student researches a different part, jotting down notes and drawing diagrams in clear view of the team members. They share their work and together create an end product that uses everyone's efforts. There is an awareness that each member is doing his or her part. Because each member has a different, missing piece, one student cannot take over the process; learners have distinct jobs that merge into a group product.

Cooperative learning, when effectively structured, can bring higher student achievement, compared to working alone or competing against one another. This is according to Marzano, Pickering, and Pollock (2001), who present a summary of research on cooperative learning. The effect size of .78 equates to a percentile gain of 28. The authors caution, however, against grouping students of low ability together too often, which can actually have a negative effect size. Johnson, Skon, and Johnson (1980) discuss the benefits lower- and medium-achieving students can get from interacting with the highest students in the class. All of the researchers here contend that the top students tend to do well in cooperative or individual settings. Their presence distributed throughout in cooperative groups, however, may tend to elevate the achievement of students around them.

How tasks are designed in the groups matters, according to Gillies and Ashman (1998). Their study investigated how students behaved and interacted when group tasks were more structured than unstructured. Not surprisingly, the students in the groups with more structure were better listeners, worked together better, were more supportive of group members, and had better learning outcomes.

Felder and Brent (2007) provide logical reasons as to why cooperative learning is so effective. Students learn better by doing something active, rather than by simply sitting and listening. In addition, they contend that weaker students, left to just work on their own, are more likely to give up when they hit a wall. However, with a group, they have some support and are more likely to push on. They also believe that cooperative learning benefits stronger students, who are put in the position of having to clarify and summarize concepts to team members, which serves to strengthen their own understandings.

Cooperative learning, then, combines the support of a team with clear structure. This structure does not diminish student control; rather, it serves to distribute it so that each student plays a critical role in the team. The absence of structure and clear roles can create the kind of "group work" that some students dislike because one member can fill the leadership vacuum and take over.

For example, here is a task with minimal structure: "Read the story in your teams and then talk about it in your groups." That task is ripe for one student to take over all of the reading and discussion. To increase student accountability, this task might be changed to

Every member will read about a half page. As you read the story, here are your individual roles: Student A will examine characters, Student B will explore the setting, Student C will trace the plot, and Student D will explain the conflict. As you read, when you see your element in the story, mark it with a sticky note and write notes. When everyone is finished, teach your part of the story elements, creating a team sticky note chart of the elements. For your group task, create with words and pictures your team's perception of the theme.

Every student has a unique job to do that morphs into the group's responsibility.

Integrating Cooperative Learning

Cooperative learning is an integral part of the active classroom. Whether it's a short processing break, checking for understanding, a new practice, or extending learning, there is a role for cooperative learning in every active lesson. Consider that students have just been taught a new concept in math, grammar, or science. It's time to determine where their understanding is at this juncture. First, on their own, students solve one problem that has been modeled (or punctuation rules or steps in a process). They now share with their partner. Together, they develop a consensus answer. Depending on time, that pair may share how they developed their answer with the neighboring pair. If a science lab is about to commence, students might first predict on their own what results will occur and then share with a partner. These predictions might now be merged into one group prediction, or the group has a dissenting opinion. Individual student whiteboards work well for these quick collaborations. A third whiteboard can be used for the consensus answers. These processing breaks provide a cognitive breather before overload kicks in. But they still follow the pattern of individual and group accountability. Students realize that they must do their part in order to achieve the group response.

Peer editing can be structured as a cooperative technique. If the writing focus is on transition words and providing supporting details, students exchange their drafts. Their partner locates transition words and details, perhaps placing small checks on the paper as they are found. Together, they might list the top three transition words from the drafts.

Students can present an overall look by completing "The number one thing we are going to develop in our writing is . . ." or "One thing I'm going to borrow from my partner's writing . . ." Students then incorporate some of those partner suggestions. (A by-product in peer editing is that the writing becomes stronger before teacher editing.) In the same vein, students creating pros and cons of a topic can switch notes and evaluate facts and reasoning. If a student knows that in a few moments a process is going to commence in which his or her thinking is going to be analyzed by a peer, that can be a motivating influence.

Cooperative learning during the work period is where students really dig in. Situated between the mini-lesson and independent work, this is the gritty, intense labor students do to prepare to stand on their own. The technique that is probably the most familiar is the jigsaw. Students leave their home teams and venture out to another place to become experts in their field. They return home, prepared to teach the rest of their team what they have learned. At the expert stations, resources are positioned. These might include hands-on experiments, reading passages, online experiences, or videos. Students take copious notes and are encouraged to visit with the other emerging experts there to best prepare themselves for their teaching. In a health class, for example, students examining the relationship between foods consumed and diseases might become an expert in one of these fields: sugar, sodium, fats, and chemical preservatives. With a simple organizer, foldable, or flip chart in hand, they proceed to their expert station and study their topic with a variety of resources. They return back to their home group and teach their portion of the lesson. Students summarize each member's short lesson on their organizer, so that all four parts of the "jigsaw" are completed when done. The teamwork now complete, students commence with individual work, synthesizing this new information into an individual piece, perhaps an ad cautioning consumers about the potential health hazards of these ingredients. (This ad could be created in the group.)

A concern some educators share about jigsawing is the amount of responsibility placed on students' shoulders to deliver the most important and accurate information to their teams. What if they pass along incorrect or incomplete information to their teams? Four things can remedy this: One consideration is using jigsawing at the most opportune time. If the concept being learned is difficult for many students to grasp, a jigsaw may not be the best fit for instructional delivery. But if students are learning about something that can be largely self-taught or is an extension of a lesson, such as different explorers or classifications of rocks, the jigsaw might be a perfect fit. Second, teacher monitoring during jigsawing is critical to address misconceptions and enhance student understanding as they are working. Third, it's helpful to provide all students the opportunity after the teach session to visit any of the resource stations to shore up any remaining gaps. And last, incorporating an individual work product, such as a summarizer, after the group effort creates an urgency to listen and utilize the information being provided.

Retell cards are a wonderful technique that incorporates a jigsaw feel but with a hands-on element. Students select cards with a topic, cause, character, battle, or plant part (whatever the learning target is today). From the success starter to the mini-lesson to the work period, students listen to everything but pay particular attention to their specific topic. For younger students, they might be listening to a story but paying close attention to one character's role. Signs are positioned around the room with the same topics. For example, if the topic is the American Civil War, one group of cards might say, "States Rights" and another, "Slavery." Matching signs are distributed on the walls around the room. If we are reading *The Giver* and students' card is the mother, their group will go into greater detail about that character. Students will pour over their notes and text, noting facts and perspectives of that particular character. In other words, students collaborate with others holding the same cards. A couple of presenters are selected. Students hold their cards and explain the story from their character's perspective, the cause they studied, the plant part, and so on. (I first saw this idea in Linda Hoyt's book *Revisit, Reflect, Retell* [2009] and have adapted it for older students. Her book is one that belongs on every reading teacher's shelf.)

Students can be provided a real-world problem to be solved with cooperative learning. For example, this problem can be posed to students: "Estimate the environmental footprint of our school for one school year and create recommendations to the Board of Education on reducing this impact." Teams first meet to make decisions about how to approach the problem and structure their work. Two students might interview someone in the accounting department to gather details of utility consumption, others might measure waste created, while others study car pool idling. They pool their data and together create recommendations from each of their "departments."

Creating a front page of a newspaper can merge deep content knowledge, writing, and artistic talents of students. There are jobs to do on a newspaper staff, including layout, illustration, and reporting. This is a small paper, so everyone is a reporter plus one other job. Of course, there's a chief editor (the team leader). There are newspaper templates online, or newsprint on tables works well. Students create news articles from the instructional target. They pretend that the event is just occurring. "Bloody Mary Burns Hundreds at Stake!" or "Junk Food Killing Citizens." A who, what, when, where, and how organizer helps students get their articles structured. After the articles are constructed, students create a name for their paper and even a tag line.

Every cooperative task does not have to be "divide and conquer." One of the most effective lessons I've created involved four tasks that each collaborative pairing had to master. They were allowed some latitude about how to best structure their work and roles and deliberated on this prior to commencing their work. For two days, teams worked in the media center together. My initial concern was how they would navigate resources such as the number of computers, resources pulled by the media specialist, primary documents, and so on within the time allowed. Their self-motivation and autonomy were simply amazing. Monitoring their progress, they mostly just wanted to share what they were learning. Over and over, I heard, "Thanks, but we got it. We don't need any help." I felt slightly guilty for getting to sit down, but it was that or continue hovering over students who were fine without me.

Structure Meets Visible Learning: Place Mats and Bow Tie Buddies

Cooperative learning is a process in which students meet face-to-face, solve problems, share work, and even merge their work into a group product. It is tactical and orderly but also highly social. Effectively facilitating the process relies on ongoing student data—seeing and hearing their thinking develop.

As a participant, it's also important to see a neighbor's work develop, to reduce the urge to rush in and take over a fellow student's portion.

Figure 6.1 uses a structure commonly called a place mat. The instructional target of the lesson was to explain ways in which animals change physical and behavior traits over time due to changing conditions, such as droughts or flooding. First, learners research their own animals. Next, students will share their results, noting commonalities. In the center, the group will merge their information to create a graphic explaining the learning target.

Place mats are an integral part of math practice. On a task typically inserted between the mini-lesson and independent work, students work out some of the "kinks" in the math they just learned. Students are provided a handful of problems to first work on their own in their space. Next, they go around the place mat and share their answers and processes. If everyone is in agreement, the consensus answer is placed in the center for that problem. If there is a disagreement, the team figures out where the process has broken

Cooperative Learning in Action

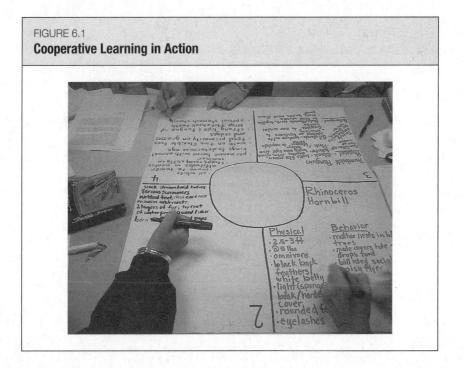

down. Now, the team examines the next problem. When progress is deemed adequate by the team and teacher, students move to independent work.

Place mats are created for four-learner teams. In the math classroom, many teachers like to pair students, rather than work in fours. For that reason, I've created an organizer called a "bow tie" (Figure 6.2). Students are placed with a "bow tie buddy" for just that day, based on current evidence. The bow tie can be placed so that students are facing one another, which reduces the tendency to just glance at a neighbor's work. They use the same process: After a couple of problems, students talk about their math, develop a consensus answer, and place it in the center. (Templates for bow ties and place mats are available at www.mathinfastlane.com.)

A strategy most teachers have used at a conference or professional development session is a carousel, sometimes called a museum walk. Carousels work well in the classroom, for practice, review, and vocabulary development. Chart paper is taped on walls around the room. Groups are arranged by color of marker so that there is a green group, a blue

FIGURE 6.2
Students Working in "Bow Tie Buddies"

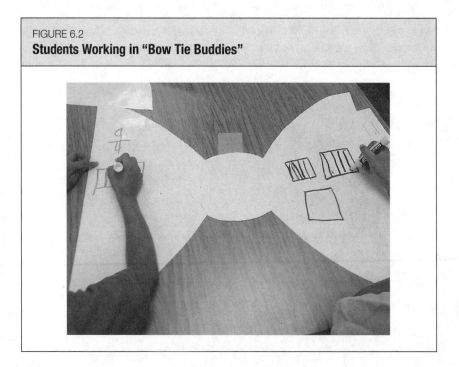

group, and so on. As with most groups, it's advisable not to exceed four members per group. Each member has a role to play, such as a scribe, illustrator, time keeper, editor, leader, or presenter. On each piece of chart paper is a task or prompt. In math, there may be a challenging word problem. In literature, characters, quotes, genres, or sentence starters might be posted. Vocabulary review becomes hands-on with this approach, as groups create their own definition and team illustration. If the purpose of the carousel is test review, there might be a mixture. Groups only have a few minutes to respond at each stop. Following their color marker, they discuss the task and respond in their team color. While students are working, clearly visible misconceptions emerge . . . a gold mine for teacher feedback. Often, a logjam occurs at one spot, signaling a considerable amount of confusion about one topic.

After they complete the carousel, everyone takes a seat, except for the presenters and perhaps one helper. Those team members examine the information at their last stop and summarize for the class. The presenters can also give a "shout out" for some exceptional or novel work, noting something interesting the green team did. Carouseling gets students moving, working together. They pick out errors in other teams' thinking. They have to summarize, edit, communicate, and practice leadership. Carouseling can extend into the next-day lesson so that all of the cycle is not completed in one day (Figure 6.3).

"Group work" has perhaps gotten a bad name. Some students are thinking, "Great, I won't have to do anything," while others have the sinking feeling that they will wind up doing it all. Cooperative learning, however, is an integral part of the active classroom. In the opening minutes, students ranking priorities or predicting what will happen in pairs or groups are learning cooperatively. A processing break in the middle of a lesson in which students pair up, compare notes, and make edits is working cooperatively. And during the student work period in which students are practicing the math they just learned with a support system, participating in literature circles with specific roles, or jigsawing the circulatory system, learning is cooperative. Students research, practice, take notes, listen, and teach one another. They are highly active. But it is structured, and teachers are right there, monitoring progress, listening to conversations, providing feedback, and—every once in a while—sitting down for just a minute.

FIGURE 6.3
Jamila Anderson, Eagle Ridge Elementary Carousel

Gillies and Boyle (2010) gathered research about teachers' experiences in implementing cooperative learning. Teachers' reflections indicated cooperative learning as a positive experience for them and their students. They also shared some challenges. First, here are some of the positive changes they noted when lessons were structured cooperatively:

- Students took more risks in learning.
- Students got to know one another.
- Learners were more relaxed.
- Students were good at time management.
- Students worked at a higher level.
- The classroom was a happier place.
- The tasks teachers created were more challenging than tasks constructed in a traditional format.

Understandably, the teachers also reflected on some hurdles in moving instruction in this direction. One was managing student socialization by making sure the talking was about the task. Interestingly, they also noted that the mindsets of the students were a challenge because they were not accustomed to working collaboratively. Of course, time to create tasks and locate resources was a concern. What they reported is, I believe, what many teachers have witnessed and worked through in developing cooperative learning tasks. The end result is so positive, however, that cooperative learning belongs in the active classroom's instructional toolbox.

Unstructured group work may not yield the benefits hoped for. Cooperative learning, on the other hand, can be a powerful instructional tool. By working on tasks that have individual, visible, and relevant goals that merge into a group result, students take greater responsibility not just for their own work but also for their team's. The group goal, or outcome, should meet the instructional target. The additional component of having students then summarize or create something on their own is from my own practice. In today's data-driven world, the question persists: "Where do each of my students' understandings reside on the learning target?" Cooperative learning, in my experience, can be highly effective in supporting students to work on their own. It is practice and student processing at its best.

Questions to Ponder

- In my next lesson, could students tactically work cooperatively?
- How can the task be created to incorporate individual and group goals?
- What sort of student grouping would best help students accomplish these goals?
- Would a framework, such as a place mat, be beneficial in structuring the work?
- What resources will be needed?
- What steps can be taken to encourage visible, ongoing work?

7

Whose Learning Is This, Anyway?

Of the pairings below, quickly determine which you feel more motivated to do, A or B.

1. A. Do problems 1–15.
   B. Select any 10 problems you'd like to do from 1 to 15.
2. A. Compare and contrast the Northern and Southern armies with a Venn diagram.
   B. Chose an effective graphic organizer to compare and contrast the Northern and Southern armies.
3. A. During your reading, you can annotate, highlight, or use sticky flags for note-taking.
   B. During your reading, underline key points.
4. A. Explain negative numbers using a football game, a bank account, or a golf game.
   B. Explain negative numbers.
5. A. We are all going to read *Romeo and Juliet*.
   B. In our study of Shakespeare, you will have the opportunity to select one of three plays to study: *Romeo and Juliet*, *Hamlet*, or *A Midsummer Night's Dream*.

Purposeful choices can motivate learners. So much of school can be a quagmire of prescribed tasks with little student ownership.

Developing autonomous learners means supporting their decision making and independent thinking, and yet, how much of their days is spent completing work just to get checked off, to avoid reprisals, or even to get a reward? Are students intrinsically excited about learning or exercising superficial compliance just to stay off the radar?

If you don't finish your work, there will be no recess. "OK, let me do the minimum to get recess." If you finish your work, you'll get some candy. "What kind of candy?"

Issues in Balancing Classroom Control

Student autonomy means that learners take some ownership and control of their education and their learning. This ownership can lead to students working with less need of external controls. They are, rather, motivated by genuine interest from within themselves, what's often referred to as intrinsic motivation. When students are intrinsically motivated to work, fewer external forces (punishments, rewards) tend to be required. Interestingly, rewards can be considered a control mechanism to get students to do work they might not want to do otherwise. "Read these books for pizza." But what happens when the pizza stops?

Extrinsic rewards and punishment are very ineffective in helping students attain academic goals; in fact, according to Deci and Ryan (1987), they might even inhibit growth. While they might control immediate student behaviors, that behavior may not continue on the next task. The researchers found that when learners got rewards just for doing something, their intrinsic motivation declined. With the possible exception of tedious tasks—things most students wouldn't want to do anyway—external motivators are ineffective. Deci, Koestner, and Ryan (2001) theorize that tasks that students may do just for rewards probably didn't inspire intrinsic motivation to begin with. We may not see stickers and candy as a control mechanism, but in a sense they are external influences that can thwart motivation. In sum, maintaining a grip on how students will participate in their own learning and then expecting students to develop as independent, motivated thinkers may be quite at odds.

Way back in 1982, Deci, Spiegel, Ryan, Koestner, and Kauffman produced some compelling research. The researchers already knew from past research that when teachers maintain more control in the classroom, rather than encourage more student autonomy, students tended to exhibit less internal motivation and self-esteem. What they sought to determine was the *cause* of teachers maintaining more control and what made teachers have this need to keep a tight grip. What they found was that when teachers were under pressure by supervisors as being the ones largely responsible for students performing up to standards, a propensity existed to exert more control over students. Teachers gave more commands to students, provided less autonomy and fewer choices to learners, and even talked more. Ironically, this pressure on teachers to reach set student outcomes had the unintended result of reducing student autonomy and choices over their own learning. Learning choices in the classroom and meaningful feedback, the researchers contend, are essential to student motivation. In classrooms in which teachers supported student autonomy, both intrinsic motivation and self-esteem increased, compared to class-rooms that were teacher-controlled. That research was in 1982. One can certainly make the case that the pressure on teachers to get their students to meet standards has increased since then.

In my own classroom experience, during professional development, and in classroom walks, I have witnessed this research. This pressure that it is on teachers' shoulders alone to increase student achievement by x percentage points may send practices in an unfortunate instruc-tional direction: more lecture, more control, more sitting, and more pushing through the learning targets. The irony, of course, is that active, student-centered learning can better serve students, but this sense that "I'd better take control of the learning to push students upward" is real.

And while pressure to get students to perform is a factor in the cre-ation of an imbalance of teacher control, it's certainly not the only one. The perceptions of students as passive recipients and teachers as expert deliverers may have become embedded from teachers' own classroom experiences—it's how many educators, parents, and grandparents were taught. And instructional habits, just like other habits, can be difficult to change. In Duhigg's 2012 book on habits, the author explains how in an effort to save energy, the brain will try to make just about any routine into a habit. The brain tends to follow the same patterns and routines, but new habits can be formed, and old habits can be changed or replaced. And, according to the author, change is easier when it occurs within a community and when the change is perceived as feasible. Of a course, students have instructional habits as well. Therefore, if learners are accustomed to a "sit 'n git" format, developing ideas on their own may be a bit of a stretch at first. Some students are comfortable in their roles as passive recipients. If listening and largely reorganizing or repeating information is an option, there might be some resistance with some students.

Hoy and Davis (2006) examined how the self-efficacy of teachers influences adolescent students. In a summary of research, they explain that teachers who perceive themselves as capable are often more open to new ideas, more likely to use instructional methods such as working in small groups and inquiry in their classrooms, and have higher expectations for students. In addition, they are often more likely to support student autonomy and provide choices. Being more confident, they are not as concerned about managing students who are working in groups or on varying tasks. They tend to be more solutions-oriented, rather than too permissive or controlling, and are even less likely to interrupt their students. Even when working with challenging students, these teachers feel less need for control and are less likely to feel personally insulted by a student's misbehavior. And, in light of the research above on how teachers may respond to increased pressure to get students to perform, more confident teachers are less likely to view this as their solitary responsibility. They are inclined to be more reflective about the strengths and weaknesses of a lesson implementation. They might even, the authors contend, confess to students, "Well, that lesson didn't go as well as I thought it would." In contrast, teachers with lower levels of confidence tend to avoid more hands-on learning due to fear of potential classroom management issues and have, in general, lower expectations for themselves and their students.

Pressure to get students to perform, instructional habits, and teacher self-efficacy can contribute to an imbalance of teacher control in the classroom. But what about school culture? Is the shared instructional mission in your building one of active learning or quiet sitting? The culture is not what's expressed on the school website but the unwritten, informal rules that teachers realize every day. At least a dozen times while facilitating professional development, this question has arisen: "Are our administrators going to be accepting of our classrooms if they walk in and students are a little noisy?" On cue, participants turn to the administrators in the room, anticipating a response. In other words, teachers want to know, If something new is tried and students are given more latitude to make decisions, and we're struggling a little bit to get the hang of more active learning, are we going to be OK? Are teachers encouraged to go out on an instructional limb or to "keep a lid on things" to limit unpredictable student behavior? Are innovative teachers celebrated, or do they tend to keep quiet during meetings to avoid rocking the boat? Because, in the same way that students have concerns about failure when giving something new a try, trying something new as a teacher carries risk as well.

Developing Student Ownership in Learning

Engaging in work that interests them for the satisfaction and enjoyment of their own performance, according to Deci, Vallerand, Pelletier, and Ryan (1991), is what intrinsically motivated learners do. The work is for their own sake, of their own volition, and not to please their teachers or parents or to gain a reward. The authors contend that there are three needs students have: competence, autonomy, and relatedness, which involves developing purposeful connections with others in the classroom. In addition, students who applied new information exhibited more motivation than those who just learned it for a test. Students with teachers who supported student autonomy were more motivated, had higher self-esteem, and felt more competent than students in classrooms with more teacher control.

To support students in becoming more genuinely motivated learners is more complex than providing rewards and punishments. Students have different interests, and one may be more intrinsically motivated in learning about artists than surface area. The student in the adjacent seat has no interest in art but is passionate about athletics. But in creating tasks and in the classroom culture, choices can be interwoven, so that their work is more interesting and valuable.

A learner presented with choices rather than mandates gets to pick how to produce his or her work. Purposeful, diverse choices pull students in. The decision is now theirs, not ours. Choices can be quite motivating. In Korb's 2012 book on motivating challenging students, he lists six top motivating learning influences. The top one is giving students more control of their learning. When students perceive that they have more control over their learning and grades, he contends that learners will become less resistant and more engaged. Consider in your own education when a piece of reading was simply mandated as required without choice or even explanation—was there a feeling of resistance, even rebellion, about doing that reading? His second motivator is lesson relevance and interest: helping students see how this new learning connects to them. Relevance and interest, of course, can be woven into choices in the classroom.

Weaving Choices Throughout Lessons

Incorporating student choices throughout a lesson may seem daunting, but it's not. Choices do not have to be in every single activity, and they don't have to be a major production. Rather, it's one piece of the classroom culture that speaks to student ownership of learning. When students are presented with choices, they are simply more open to jumping in and learning. Students get to make decisions, which they enjoy. Choices incorporate variety, varying interests, student strengths, and learning preferences. But students also have areas of weakness that need to be remedied, so there are times that options may be more limited.

Choices in the Opening Minutes

The opening few minutes of a lesson, as discussed earlier, are hugely important. Students are provided opportunities to connect prior knowledge to new incoming information, a strategy that not only makes learning easier for students but also facilitates storage in long-term memory (Willis, 2006). Students are also making decisions about the level of engagement they are willing to risk. And, of course, the learning target is articulated. Providing choices can further enhance student motivation during this critical time in the lesson.

For example, if students are about to embark on a lesson about distinguishing the differences between invertebrates and vertebrates, the opener might be to have a slide show of pictures, such as sponges, amphibians, worms, and fish. Students develop ideas on their own or with a partner how these animals are alike and different to create their own two classifications. Now, students can select any four additional animals and place them in the appropriate categories. At this juncture, learners have the option of adjusting their original labels. Next, they can choose one person at a neighboring table with whom to trade responses. Last, students will compare their work with what biologists call invertebrates and vertebrates. This simple opener provided students with a measure of autonomy: working alone or with a partner, choosing other animals to study, creating categories, and selecting someone with whom to share. Compare this approach with choices to "Today, we're going to study invertebrates and vertebrates."

If students began studying the circulatory system yesterday, and the opener will serve to link yesterday's learning to today's target, consider using a quick write. These writings provide students with a moment to reflect on what they have learned and create something short in their own words. For this example, students may have these options: Create a picture that shows the relationship among the three parts of the circulatory system, create an introduction for a news broadcast, or create a sports analogy (gymnastics is like the circulatory system because . . .) for the system with a brief explanation. After the writing, students select a student at an adjacent table for feedback. In these choices, students who are drawn to visual imagery have an option, as well as more auditory learners, and most students have an interest in some sport. In addition, they can select a friendly face for feedback.

Choices in the Work Period

Paired readings can be implemented many ways. Teachers can incorporate oral reading, silent reading, and choral readings. Students can select different roles, such as the scribe and the highlighter or the figurative language expert and the character development tracker. Paired readings can also include a road map with choices woven in, such as this portion of one for the first chapter of *The Lord of the Flies,* by William Golding. Readers are given the option of the character they would like to study, the quotes they feel are representative of their characters, and even how they would like to read the passage. Examples of choices are set in boldface:

Readers will **select a character** of focus, Piggy or Ralph. **Select** two highlighter colors to represent the characters. Read pages 7, 8, and 9 **silently or together**. Scour the text for information **you deem most valuable** in explaining your character. Next, compare and contrast with your partner the two characters. Together, create **either a Facebook or LinkedIn profile** for the character of your choosing.

	Ralph	Piggy
Physical characteristics		
Backstory/history		
Descriptive quotes		
Reactions to situations		

In examining the setting, readers might select their top five adjectives and two nouns the author used. In responding to reading, students can choose a character they find most intriguing for a character and me comparison. They can compare the theme of their current study to any work they have read in the past.

And, while there is a shared literary enjoyment teachers and readers get from reading the same works, students should have many opportunities to select their own readings. Every teacher has favorite pieces of literature and truly cherishes sharing these works with students. But students need to also discover *their* favorites, which might be quite different from their teacher's. A good conversation to have with every student in the building is, "What are you currently reading?" In one building in which I consulted, teachers took a reading interest survey along with students. Students and teachers were matched according to the survey for reading groups that met one morning per week. Students who were comic book aficionados met with teachers who shared that passion; others read vampire novels. But even when a class is reading the same work, choices in how they read and respond are critical to the enjoyment of literature.

Using Menus for Student Work

Menus, sometimes called choice boards, are versatile tools for the student work period, homework, and even assessments. Menus have many looks; some are even constructed like restaurant menus, with appetizers, entrées, and desserts. The purpose of menus is to give students the intellectual freedom to explore a topic in different ways. They offer choices, interest, and learning style propensities within a structure. Menus, in my experience, are an exceptional instructional tool, with a few provisos:

- They should extend over one or two days, not weeks. Novelty, high interest, and choices are what makes these work, and if students are entrenched for too lengthy of a time period, interest can wane. They can start to feel like a worksheet instead of a captivating experience.
- Menus must be constructed so that options are designed to master the learning target. Therefore, whatever choices students select should enable an entrenchment in learning goals. So, after creating the menu, it's a good idea to examine all possibilities students may choose to validate that successful completion of these tasks will indeed meet the learning target.
- Have a plan for absent students, especially if classroom resources are required for the menu.

In the block menu in Figure 7.1, students are given the task of describing three principles: federalism, separation of powers, and checks and balances. This menu would be used as an acquisition lesson. Students would use multiple resources, and points are distributed equally based on the requirements of the standard. Other menus might have a range of points, depending on the difficulty of the task or weight of the concept. Students can begin anywhere they like and may select any of the options. Notice that the options have a range of interests and learning styles, but every option requires students to describe the principles, which is the learning target.

In addition to the benefits of choice, student interest, and autonomy that menus offer learners, the implementation of these in the classroom can provide rich opportunities for immediate feedback and improvement. During class implementation, learners complete components at varying

FIGURE 7.1
Sample Menu for History

Learning target: Describe the principles of federalism, separation of powers, and checks and balances.

Principle	Option 1	Option 2	Option 3	Points
Federalism	Create a Venn diagram comparing national and state powers.	Create a PowerPoint slide describing key points of federalism.	Create a finger puppet phone video describing federalism.	/25
Separation of Powers	Create a collage describing separation of powers.	Write a page of a children's book describing separation of powers.	Explain separation of powers by substituting song lyrics.	/25
Checks & Balances	Write a Facebook post describing checks and balances.	Create a graphic organizer describing checks and balances.	Create a sticky note sculpture depicting checks and balances.	/25
Put It Together	Create a cube game with all three principles. Play at your table.	Create a sort with all three principles. Share with a partner.	Create a flip-book with all three principles.	/25

times. I encourage them to share their work on an ongoing basis. In this way, conversations are had that may improve their work. Students can decide whether they want to improve the work for additional points. Most, when given the option, make changes immediately and gain more points. This quick, descriptive feedback moves learning, and students see progress and point accumulations right away. Menus, particularly when they are of short duration, give students more control not just of their learning but of their grades. In fact, I have personally never had one student make a failing grade on a menu.

Math menus, by their nature, will have practice problems, but those can vary by interest and degree of difficulty, and point values adjust for difficulty. Math menus can also incorporate vocabulary and writing. In the sample in Figure 7.2, the 20-point problems are for students who still need practice. The middle row incorporates writing or drawing, offering students some options of how to explain fraction number sense. The last row is the most difficult, but students can receive up to 60 points. In this sample, students cannot reach 100 without venturing into more difficult tasks.

Choices don't have to come in the form of menus, but they offer a thoughtful way for learners to display their understandings in various

---

FIGURE 7.2

Sample Menu for Math

Learning target: Demonstrate your understanding of fraction number sense.
Mix and match boxes to equal 100 potential points.

1. 1/8 + 4/5 2. 9/10 + 7/8 3. 3/5 + 3/4 + 1/8	1. 3/4 – 1/3 2. 1 1/12 – 3/4 3. 1 1/2 – 9/10	1. 2 3/4 – 1 2. 5 1/2 – 1 3/4 3. 4 3/4 – 2 3/4	20 Points
Your friend Mark added 1/2 and 3/4 and got an answer of 4/6. Write him a note explaining where he went wrong.	Create a series of steps to solve this problem: 5 2/3 – 1 3/4	Draw models that display this problem: 5 3/4 – 1 3/4	40 Points
Building a Garden John needs 2 feet of border to go around his flower garden. He has two pieces of border. One is 7/8 of a foot long, and the other is 8/7 feet long. Estimate whether he has enough border. Explain.	**Running** Jessie wants to run 1 mile today. He runs 1/2 mile to Mike's house and 1/3 mile to Nick's. Did he run more or less than a mile? How much?	**Picking Berries** Sharon picked 3 3/4 quarts of blueberries and 4 1/3 quarts of raspberries. How many quarts did she pick?	60 Points

ways and even provide some student control over their grades. Unit tests can even be constructed using menus.

Below are ideas for menus tasks. Rather than ask students to simply write a summary, they can

- Create a LinkedIn profile, a mock journal entry, or an obituary for a historical figure.
- Create a business plan or just a business card.
- Create a brochure, poster, flyer, or advertisement.
- Write a letter to the editor or a letter to a friend in the next classroom.
- Take a stand in a persuasive essay or a write a news article.
- Create a survey.
- Create one page of a screenplay (one minute).

For more tactile tasks and visual tasks, students can

- Create a math card game (such as red cards are negative, black are positive).
- Create flash cards.

- Create a crossword puzzle.
- Create a hand outline with five key facts.
- Create a clay sculpture as a metaphor.
- Create a graphic organizer or picture.

Whether it's multiple resources, varied writing prompts, choices of projects, or even the order in which students proceed with their work, choices are a key motivator in students wanting to genuinely engage in their work.

Closing Minutes

The lesson is ending, and students need to demonstrate progress on their learning target. If students have been practicing multiplication of fractions by a whole number, for example, they might select one last problem that relates to sports, shopping, or farming. If students have wrapped up their menus, they have perhaps generated enough evidence of learning that they can just select one or two items to share. In addition to the lesson close, there's another piece that's helpful in building student autonomy: feedback on how the lesson worked for students.

Consider practically every restaurant or online shopping experience: It seems that every business is desperate for customer feedback. In fact, they offer prizes and discounts just for taking their survey. Why? Companies want to know more about their customers' experiences to improve the business. It's certainly not warranted every day, but periodically it's a good idea to gauge the pulse of the classroom experience. So, in the last couple of minutes, ask students to express how the lesson worked for them today:

- On a scale of 1 to 5, how was the learning experience for you today?
- On a sticky, tell the part of the lesson that was most helpful and one thing that didn't work as well.
- On a sticky, write me a note about how this lesson worked today.
- Rate this lesson like a movie, with 1 to 5 stars, and write one thing that you want me to know.
- Finish this thought: "My biggest concern about today's lesson is _____."
- Finish these thoughts: "I'm good on this: _____. I could use some help on this: _____."

Providing choices for student learning is one way to promote student ownership of their own learning. Rather than an entirely teacher-selected list of tasks, students get to be in charge of some of their experiences. To stick to an imposed list of teacher-created tasks can then necessitate more external controls, such as rewards and punishments, to prod students into compliance. The active classroom is one of developing greater student autonomy so that more of their work is of their own volition.

Motivating students is always a hot topic for educators. Rather than creating elaborate reward programs or giving them stickers, the research leads us to another place: give them purposeful choices with relevant tasks they really enjoy doing.

Questions to Ponder

- In our classrooms or schools, is there an overreliance on extrinsic motivators?
- In our lesson plans, are choices woven in to provide more student control?
- As part of our instructional routines, are we providing avenues for students to tell us how our lessons are working for them?

8

Barriers and Big Picture

In a 2014 survey by the employee engagement firm TINYpulse, more than 200,000 employees in more than 500 organizations were asked what motivated them. They were given 10 possible answers from which to choose. Money, a clearly extrinsic motivator, came in seventh. The number one response workers selected was peer motivation and camaraderie. Employee comments on that topic referenced a sense of obligation not to let their peers down—a sense of responsibility to the group, that they were all in this together. The second-highest response was an intrinsic desire to do a good job. Feeling recognized and making an impact were next.

Consider the potential similarities of what motivates many students to work: the importance of the task, collaborating with and a feeling of belonging in a group, the sense of being competent at a job. In both, extrinsic motivation—rewards—ranked much further behind. In some ways, students' motivational needs are akin to ours.

The commentary of the report mentioned that hiring managers make efforts to select only employees who can work well collaboratively, are good at communication, and can share praise. A clear benefit of organizations is they can handpick employees who are the best fit for their mission. Similarly, educators in school districts are selected who will best contribute to the mission of a school. Other applicants were not picked. You were.

The classroom is quite different. Teachers rarely get to select students. Rather, we cultivate, develop, and nurture those assigned to us to become the type of people employers and universities will seek. Students' work spaces (our classrooms) can be crowded, with barely enough room to squeeze in enough desks. And some of the content hardly inspires intrinsic motivation. A few students do bounce into class passionate about learning about pollination or the Russian Revolution or which of Henry's wives kept their heads. Most are more intrigued by their phones.

The student-centered classroom can enhance student motivation and authentic engagement. In the student-centered culture, these practices prevail:

- Time is carved out each day for students to practice, collaborate, and create meaningful work.
- Students make meaningful decisions about work processes and outcomes.
- Students feel like they belong.
- Ongoing opportunities for feedback prevail based on their developing, open work.
- Over the course of a unit, students talk more than teachers.
- Work is valuable, interesting, and relevant.
- Students are not just learners; they are collectors of evidence on their progress.
- Over the course of a unit, students are provided opportunities to learn via different channels.
- Rewards and reprisals are sparsely used; rather, students are largely motivated from within, due to the nature of the tasks.
- Over the course of a unit, students are often engaged at a higher level of thinking, with teachers understanding that students also need foundational information.
- Students develop a sense of autonomy and accomplishment about their work.
- Students are provided opportunities for leadership and managerial roles.
- Learning is directed by clear, explicit learning targets.

Challenges and Solutions in the Active Classroom

There are challenges to transitioning to a classroom in which students can get up to grab a resource, confer with a team member, and make some of their own decisions about their work. In Gillies and Boyle's research (2010) mentioned in Chapter 6, teachers they studied realized impressive benefits from implementing cooperative learning, such as a higher level of work and reduced student anxiety. They also talked about challenges, such as managing student socialization, time, and resources. I have found that these three barriers that teachers identified are somewhat universal.

It bears mention, although perhaps an obvious point, that students, teachers, and leaders are at varying degrees of implementation. For a teacher in a pattern and mindset of largely delivery, the first step might be to implement these four things first: the success starter to link prior knowledge and inspire curiosity, standards walls to articulate learning targets, small cognitive fatigue breaks for students in which they can share ideas with a partner and perhaps develop a solution together, and a menu with choices. After a few lessons, the next step might be to try a cooperative technique, such as a jigsaw, that has a comfortable level of structure but has students moving and talking. For an educator with some degree of confidence in this arena, stations or group problem solving might be a next step. For every educator, it's important to realize that when trying new strategies in the classroom, things don't always go perfectly—tweaking is inevitable. Reflect on changes that need to be made and move on.

There is a predictability and structure to the student-centered classroom, but there is also variety within that structure. Structure and passivity are not synonymous. In every lesson, students begin with something compelling to tap into prior knowledge, and an explicit learning target is identified. There is a time to listen to a lesson, but that lesson is chunked appropriately with quick, soft formative assessments. Students have time to work, typically together in the beginning of the work period. These tasks prepare students to work individually, which often involves choices by the student. Feedback is ongoing because work is highly open for all to see. The lesson always concludes with students, peers, and the teacher looking at progress toward the learning targets. So, within the lesson framework, there is reliability and structure but also novelty. Some content is perfect for stations; other content is just right for cooperative learning.

A thoughtful, well-constructed lesson of appropriate challenge with high-interest tasks can proactively alleviate much off-task behavior of students but not all of it. Even the most fabulously compelling lesson requires classroom procedures that need to be addressed so that work can get done expeditiously. Here are some pragmatic pointers for managing the active classroom:

- Have materials already out. Passing out papers and other materials encourages students to get fidgety. They want to get started, and another team inevitably gets resources first. Assign students as material managers to get materials back in folders for upcoming groups. Resist fighting the "pencil wars." Have a system in place for students to check writing materials out.
- Greet every student at the door by name. Tell them it's good to see them, how great class is going to be, or how you think they will find the lesson interesting—something genuine.
- Start class immediately. Every building has specific lesson expectations, but typically it's a good idea to get the success starter going and then check attendance while they are working.
- Plan transitions and student movement. Examine the lesson in terms of where students will be and how furniture can be arranged. For example, if students are going to work in groups, it might be best to have the students sit in groups during the success starter rather than move minutes later. It's helpful to have stations numbered, groups already named with the first station number, and instructions already there. Give students a signal that movement is about to begin.
- Before embarking on a lesson in which there will be quite a bit of talking or movement, consider reviewing expectations for voice volume and team norms.
- When implementing stations for the first time, consider not having a teacher station. This will facilitate monitoring every center. Provide opportunities to review expectations as needed to individual students.

- Have a contingency plan for students who do not behave appropriately during the lesson. There can be a table where they can work alone for a while and then try again with their group.
- Incorporate a variety of materials at different levels and learning channels to encourage on-task behavior.
- Resist talking over students when they get noisy. Consider a break from action to reinforce expectations.
- Encourage students in their work, provide feedback on the task, and commend hard work and a job well done.

The Issue of Time

Lessons that are thought-provoking in which students invest in their learning often take more time to create. The payoff is having rewarding days with students. Time planning compelling lessons can result in fewer discipline issues, which can result in teachers having to allocate less time for parent contacts, office referrals, and getting work ready for students who have been removed from class. So putting the time and work in up front in creating student-centered lessons may just free up time from disciplinary tasks.

But teacher time is already at a premium. Teachers are more likely than other professionals to do additional work at home. According to economist Rachel Krantz-Kent (2008) of the Bureau of Labor Statistics, on an average workday, 30 percent of American teachers already do extra work at home. And 51 percent of teachers work on Sundays. Not surprisingly, teachers are also more likely than other professionals to work a second job. A survey of working habits of teachers in England done by its Department for Education (2014) revealed that teachers, on average, work about 50 hours a week, including about 12 hours a week outside of work.

Therefore, rather than pile on more hours, schools may want to seek solutions to reallocate time by examining how teachers' time is currently being used. Because if the expectation is to have learning experiences that genuinely involve students at a higher rate of thinking, that takes time.

A starting point may be to survey teachers about where time is being spent and ideas for coordinating or reducing some things currently in action. Every building has different schedules and needs, but here are some potential starting points:

- Meetings: Are all meetings essential? Are they appropriate in length? Does everyone need to attend? Do meetings have agendas with tight time lines with strict adherence?
- Teacher noninstructional duties: Can lunch, hallway, or other duties be periodically covered by administrators to allocate more time for planning? In general, are noninstructional responsibilities so weighty that they are infringing too much on teacher planning time?
- Is technology being maximized to support teachers in parent contacts, grading, and other areas?
- Class coverage: Can substitute teacher funds be used so that teachers have periodic planning sessions? Can a full day prior to the start of the semesters be incorporated for planning so that students begin with highly effective lessons?
- Are there support people who can help teachers in planning efforts? Some things require the sole attention of the teachers, such as vetting resources and creating learning targets. But after the lesson is planned, there are many pieces that could be handled by others, such as cutting sorts and making copies. Can parent volunteers, student teachers, or others assist teachers in these areas?

The Big Picture

When I was a lead teacher in a building, I did something that was not particularly innovative, but it was meaningful. I randomly selected a student's schedule with a plan of spending the day as our students did. The goal I established myself was to see if we were realizing the lofty missions we had established on paper and our website in actual classrooms. I only made it for two hours.

These were committed, highly professional, content-rich teachers who arrived early and stayed late to tutor. In every class, more and more information pounded at my head. The first teacher talked and talked, and more and more academic vocabulary words floated around the room. At the sound of the buzzer, I shuffled down the hall to the next class. More and more talking and copying. The desk was so hard that my back ached. I desperately needed to stretch my legs but remained upright. My eyes became heavy from the onslaught of information. A burgeoning sense of claustrophobia crept in. I kept thinking, "We're going to get a break soon, right?" I looked at our students and marveled at their degree of disciplined compliance. I didn't have it in me. I bailed because I had a choice.

Students have so few choices. The bus comes at the same time every day to the same school. They file into our classrooms. What awaits them instructionally is up to us.

Stacks of research support the benefits of getting students more authentically engaged in their own learning. Unfortunately, research also continues to lament that most classrooms are still locked in a largely teacher delivery mode.

Years ago, I was setting up for professional development one afternoon in the cafeteria of a large high school. Two students were hanging out. They were curious about what teachers would be doing. I explained that teachers continue learning about effective instructional practices all through their careers. I asked them to tell me one thing they would like their teachers to know. Without even a pause, one said this: "Tell them that they just keep going on and on when we don't even know what they are talking about half the time. They need to stop once in a while." I've never forgotten his advice.

So, in his words, let's stop going on and on. Instead, let's give students rich opportunities to practice, put their heads together, lead, move, talk, and explore. Let *them* make some decisions about their own learning. Let *them* discover the most interesting parts of the content on their own. Let's put *them* in the fast lane of learning.

References

Althoff, S. E., Linde, K. J., Mason, J. D., Nagel, N. M., & O'Reilly, K. A. (2007). *Learning objectives: Posting and communicating daily learning objectives to increase student achievement and motivation* [Action research case]. Chicago: Saint Xavier University. Retrieved from http://files.eric.ed.gov/fulltext/ED496125.pdf

Ames, C. (1992). Classrooms: Goals, structures, and student motivation. *Journal of Educational Psychology, 84*(3), 261–271.

Bailey, F., & Pransky, K. (2014). *Memory at work in the classroom: Strategies to help underachieving students.* Alexandria, VA: ASCD.

Brown, J. E. (2007, August 21). *Building rigor into every lesson in every classroom* [Presentation]. Department of Curriculum, Instruction, and School Leadership.

Bullard, L., Felder, R., & Raubenheimer, D. (2008). Effects of active learning on student performance and retention. *Proceedings from the Annual Conference of the American Society for Engineering Education.* Retrieved from http://www4.ncsu.edu/unity/lockers/users/f/felder/public/Papers/ASEE08(ActiveLearning).pdf

California Department of Education. (2000). *History–social science content standards for California public schools, kindergarten through grade twelve.* Retrieved from http://www.cde.ca.gov/be/st/ss/documents/histsocscistnd.pdf

Cross, J. S., & Nagle, J. M. (1969). Teachers talk too much! *The English Journal, 58*(9), 1362–1365.

Cwiek, S. (2014, January 27). The middle class took off 100 years ago . . . thanks to Henry Ford? *NPR.* Retrieved from http://www.npr.org/2014/01/27/267145552/the-middle-class-took-off-100-years-ago-thanks-to-henry-ford

Davies, A. (2007). Involving students in the classroom assessment process. In D. Reeves (Ed.), *Ahead of the curve: The power of assessment to transform teaching and learning* (pp. 31–57). Bloomington, IN: Solution Tree.

Dean, C. B., Hubbell, E. R., Pitler, H., & Stone, B. (2012). *Classroom instruction that works: Research-based strategies for increasing student achievement* (2nd ed.). Alexandria, VA: ASCD; and Denver, CO: McREL.

Deci, E. L., Koestner, R., & Ryan, R. M. (2001). Extrinsic rewards and intrinsic motivation in education: Reconsidered once again. *Review of Educational Research, 71*(1), 1–27.

Deci, E. L., & Ryan, R. M. (1987). The support of autonomy and the control of behavior. *Journal of Personality and Social Psychology, 53*(6), 1024–1037.

Deci, E. L., Spiegel, N. H., Ryan, R. M., Koestner, R., & Kauffman, M. (1982). Effects of performance standards on teaching styles: Behavior of controlling teachers. *Journal of Educational Psychology, 74*(6), 852–859.

Deci, E. L., Vallerand, R. J., Pelletier, L. G., & Ryan, R. M. (1991). Motivation and education: The self-determination perspective. *Educational Psychologist, 26*(3–4), 325–346.

DeLeon, J. E., & Borchers, R. E. (1998). High school graduate employment trends and the skills graduates need to enter Texas manufacturing industries. *Journal of Career and Technical Education, 15*(1), 28–41.

Department for Education. (2014). Teachers' workload diary survey 2013 [Research report]. Retrieved from https://www.gov.uk/government/uploads/system/uploads/attachment_data/file/285941/DFE-RR316.pdf

Duckworth, A. L., Peterson, C., Matthews, M. D., & Kelly, D. R. (2007). Grit: Perseverance and passion for long-term goals. *Journal of Personality and Social Psychology, 92*(6), 1087–1101.

Duhigg, C. (2012). *The power of habit: Why we do what we do in life and business.* New York: Random House.

Eccles, J. S., Wigfield, A., Midgley, C., Reuman, D., Mac Iver, D., & Feldlaufer, H. (1993). Negative effects of traditional middle schools on students' motivation. *The Elementary School Journal, 93*(5), 553–574.

Felder, R. M., & Brent, R. (2007). Cooperative learning. In P. A. Mabrouk (Ed.), *Active learning: Models from the analytical sciences* (pp. 34–53). Washington, DC: American Chemical Society.

Freeman, S., Eddy, S. L., McDonough, M., Smith, M. K., Okoroafor, N., Jordt, H., & Wenderoth, M. P. (2014). Active learning increases student performance in science, engineering, and mathematics. *Proceedings of the National Academy of Sciences, 111*(23), 8410–8415.

Gillies, R. M., & Ashman, A. F. (1998). Behavior and interactions of children in cooperative groups in lower and middle elementary grades. *Journal of Educational Psychology, 90*(4), 746–757.

Gillies, R. M., & Boyle, M. (2010). Teachers' reflections on cooperative learning: Issues of implementation. *Teaching and Teacher Education, 26*(4), 933–940.

Gladwell, M. (2013). *David and Goliath: Underdogs, misfits, and the art of battling giants.* New York: Little, Brown and Company.

Gupta, S. (2015). Is sitting the new smoking? *CNN.* Retrieved from http://www.cnn.com/videos/health/2015/04/09/cnn-orig-living-to-100-how-sitting-can-hurt-you.cnn/video/playlists/living-to-100/

Gurian, M., & Stevens, K. (2004). With boys and girls in mind. *Educational Leadership, 62*(3), 21–26. Retrieved from http://www.ascd.org/publications/educational-leadership/nov04/vol62/num03/With-Boys-and-Girls-in-Mind.aspx

Hansen, D. A. (1989). Lesson evading and lesson dissembling: Ego strategies in the classroom. *American Journal of Education, 97*(2), 184–208.

Hartley, J., & Davies, I. K. (1978). Note taking: A critical review. *Programmed Learning and Educational Technology, 15*(3), 207–224.

Hattie, J. (2009). *Visible learning: A synthesis of over 800 meta-analyses relating to achievement.* New York: Routledge.

Hattie, J. (2012). *Visible learning for teachers: Maximizing impact on learning.* New York: Routledge.

Hattie, J., & Timperley, H. (2007). The power of feedback. *Review of Educational Research, 77*(1), 81–112.

Hattie, J., & Yates, G. (2014). *Visible learning and the science of how we learn.* New York: Routledge.

Hoy, A. H., & Davis, H. A. (2006). Teacher self-efficacy and its influence on the achievement of adolescents. In F. Pajares & T. Urdan (Eds.), *Self-efficacy beliefs of adolescents* (pp. 117–137). Greenwich, CT: Information Age Pubishing.

Hoyt, L. (2009). *Revisit, reflect, retell: Time-tested strategies for teaching reading comprehension.* Portsmouth, NH: Heinemann.

Hull, T. H., Miles, R. H., & Balka, D. S. (2014). *Realizing rigor in the mathematics classroom.* Thousand Oaks, CA: Corwin Press.

James, J. (2011, April 10). High school students sit for too long, new health research suggests. *Peninsula Press.* Retrieved from http://archive.peninsulapress.com/2011/04/10/high-school-students-sit-for-too-long-new-health-research-suggests/

Jaschik, S. (2015). Well-prepared in their own eyes. *Inside Higher Ed.* Retrieved from https://www.insidehighered.com/news/2015/01/20/study-finds-big-gaps-between-student-and-employer-perceptions

Jensen, E. (2005). *Teaching with the brain in mind* (2nd ed.). Alexandria, VA: ASCD.

Johnson, D., & Johnson, R. (2009). An educational psychology success story: Social interdependence theory and cooperative learning. *Educational Researcher, 38*(5), 365–379.

Johnson, D. W., Skon, L., & Johnson, R. (1980). Effects of cooperative, competitive, and individualistic conditions on children's problem-solving performance. *American Educational Research Journal, 17*(1), 83–93.

Kirschner, P. A., Sweller, J., & Clark, R. E. (2006). Why minimal guidance during instruction does not work: An analysis of the failure of constructivist, discovery, problem-based, experiential, and inquiry-based teaching. *Educational Psychologist, 41*(2), 75–86.

Korb, R. (2012). *Motivating defiant and disruptive students to learn: Positive classroom management strategies.* Thousand Oaks, CA: Corwin Press.

Krantz-Kent, R. (2008). Teachers' work patterns: When, where, and how much do U.S. teachers work? *Monthly Labor Review.* Retrieved from http://www.bls.gov/opub/mlr/2008/03/art4full.pdf

Levy, F., & Rodkin, J. (2015). The Bloomberg recruiter report: Job skills companies want but can't get. *Bloomberg.* Retrieved from http://www.bloomberg.com/graphics/2015-job-skills-report/

Marzano, R. J. (2004). *Building background knowledge for academic achievement: Research on what works in schools.* Alexandria, VA: ASCD.

Marzano, R. J. (2007). *The art and science of teaching: A comprehensive framework for effective instruction.* Alexandria, VA: ASCD.

Marzano, R. J., Pickering, D. J., & Pollock, J. E. (2001). *Classroom instruction that works: Research-based strategies for increasing student achievement.* Alexandria, VA: ASCD; and Denver, CO: McREL.

Marzano, R. J., & Toth, M. D. (2014). *Teaching for rigor: A call for a critical instructional shift.* Learning Sciences Marzano Center Monograph. York, PA: Learning Sciences International.

Movitz, A. P., & Holmes, K. P. (2007). Finding center: How learning centers evolved in a secondary, student-centered classroom. *English Journal, 96*(3), 68–73.

National Association of Colleges and Employers. (2014, November 12). Job outlook: The candidate skills/qualities employers want, the influence of attributes. Retrieved from http://www.naceweb.org/s11122014/job-outlook-skills-qualities-employers-want.aspx

National Council of Teachers of Mathematics. (2014). *Principles to actions: Ensuring mathematical success for all.* Reston, VA: Author.

Nuthall, G. (1999). The way students learn: Acquiring knowledge from an integrated science and social studies unit. *The Elementary School Journal, 99*(4), 303–341.

Osterman, K. F. (2000). Students' need for belonging in the school community. *Review of Educational Research, 70*(3), 323–367.

Owen, N., Sparling, P. B., Healy, G. N., Dunstan, D. W., & Matthews, C. E. (2010). Sedentary behavior: Emerging evidence for a new health risk. *Mayo Clinic Proceedings, 85*(12), 1138–1141. Retrieved from http://www.mayoclinicproceedings.org/article/S0025-6196(11)60368-6/pdf

Riskowski, J. L., Todd, C. D., Wee, B., Dark, M., & Harbor, J. (2009). Exploring the effectiveness of an interdisciplinary water resources engineering module in an eighth grade science course. *International Journal of Engineering Education, 25*(1), 181–195.

Rollins, S. P. (2014). *Learning in the fast lane: 8 ways to put all students on the road to success.* Alexandria, VA: ASCD.

Slavin, R. E. (1983). When does cooperative learning increase student achievement? *Psychological Bulletin, 94*(3), 429–445.

Slavin, R. E. (1991). Synthesis of research on cooperative learning. *Educational Leadership, 38*(8), 655–660.

Sousa, D. A. (2008). *How the brain learns mathematics.* Thousand Oaks, CA: Corwin Press.

Stanley, T. J. (2000). *The millionaire mind.* Kansas City, MO: Andrews McMeel Publishing.

Stefanou, C. R., Perencevich, K. C., DiCintio, M., & Turner, J. C. (2004). Supporting autonomy in the classroom: Ways teachers encourage student decision making and ownership. *Educational Psychologist, 39*(2), 97–110. Retrieved from http://faculty.washington.edu/sunolen/562/old%20562%20files/Stefanou.pdf

TINYpulse. (2014). The 7 key trends impacting today's workplace: Results from the 2014 TINYpulse employee engagement and organizational culture report. Retrieved from http://cdn2.hubspot.net/hub/443262/file-2492854670-pdf/Employee_Engagement__Organizational_Culture_Report.pdf?t=1434127674349

Tomlinson, C. A. (2001). *How to differentiate instruction in mixed-ability classrooms* (2nd ed.). Alexandria, VA: ASCD.

Tsegaye, A. G., & Davidson, L. M. (2014). The ratio of teacher talking time to students talking time in EFL classroom: A case in six partner preparatory schools of Haramaya University, Ethiopia. *Abhinav National Monthly Refereed Journal of Research in Arts and Education, 3*(5), 1–5.

Van de Pol, J., Volman, M., & Beishuizen, J. (2010). Scaffolding in teacher-student interaction: A decade of research. *Educational Psychology Review, 22*(3), 271–296.

Wallinger, L. (2012, July 1). *Effective strategies to include rigor in classroom instruction* [Presentation]. Virginia Department of Education.

Willis, J. (2006). *Research-based strategies to ignite student learning: Insights from a neurologist and classroom teacher.* Alexandria, VA: ASCD.

Wolfe, P. (2010). *Brain matters: Translating research into classroom practice* (2nd ed.). Alexandria, VA: ASCD.

Yair, G. (2000). Educational battlefields in America: The tug-of-war over students' engagement with instruction. *Sociology of Education, 73*(4), 247–269.

Index

The letter *f* following a page number denotes a figure.

About the Author

 **Suzy Pepper Rollins** is a passionate lifelong educator whose mission is to create academic success for ALL learners by embedding instructional practices that create energized, autonomous, focused learners. A national presenter across subject areas, she is the founder of Math in the Fast Lane (www.mathinfastlane.com), an online instructional resource for grades 3–8 teachers. In addition, she has embarked on a new project called MyEdExpert.com, which is a community of education experts who share research-based work with schools.

Rollins is the author of *Learning in the Fast Lane* (ASCD, 2014); this is her second book. She can be reached at suzyprollins@gmail.com.

Related ASCD Resources

At the time of publication, the following ASCD resources were available (ASCD stock numbers in parentheses). For up-to-date information about ASCD resources, go to www.ascd.org. Search the complete archives of *Educational Leadership* at www.ascd.org/el.

ASCD EDge®

Exchange ideas and connect with other educators interested in active learning on the social networking site ASCD EDge® at http://ascdedge.ascd.org/.

Print Products

Learning in the Fast Lane: 8 Ways to Put All Students on the Road to Academic Success by Suzy Pepper Rollins (#114026)

Cultivating Curiosity in K–12 Classrooms: How to Promote and Sustain Deep Learning by Wendy L. Ostroff (#116001)

The Formative Five: Fostering Grit, Empathy, and Other Success Skills Every Student Needs by Thomas R. Hoerr (#116043)

Learning to Choose, Choosing to Learn: The Key to Student Motivation and Achievement by Mike Anderson (#116015)

The Motivated Brain: Improving Student Attention, Engagement, and Perseverance by Gayle Gregory and Martha Kaufeldt (#115041)

Real Engagement: How do I help my students become motivated, confident, and self-directed learners? (ASCD Arias) by Allison Zmuda and Robyn R. Jackson (#SF115056)

PD Online® Courses

Total Participation Techniques (#PD15OC007M)

For more information: send e-mail to member@ascd.org; call 1-800-933-2723 or 703-578-9600, press 2; send a fax to 703-575-5400; or write to Information Services, ASCD, 1703 N. Beauregard St., Alexandria, VA 22311-1714 USA.